Purposeful Development of Professional Learning Processes

Considerations for Pedagogy, Research and Practice

Editor

Michael Ladick

Associate Editors

Charity Gamboa Embley, Crystal Rose, Shona Rose

Assistant Editor

Elizabeth Davis Jones

ISBN 978-1-64504-250-1 (Paperback)

ISBN 978-1-64504-251-8 (Hardback)

ISBN 978-1-64504-252-5 (E-Book)

Library of Congress Control Number: 2022935628

Printed on acid-free paper

DIO Press International Editorial Board

Table of Contents

Preface

A consistent theme throughout this book focuses on how all of the authors believe that professional learning begins with the self in some form. Those who are willing to dabble in professional learning exercises educationally evolve, choosing to obtain a deeper understanding of one's decision-making abilities over outcomes. Professional learners address and overcome personal educational pitfalls while creating relationships, collaborating, and obtaining feedback from those within and outside their immediate educational infrastructure (Admiraal et al., 2019). Additionally, professional learners are wise to not center their development on a single moment within an event, but on the series of trials and tribulations that have been collectively recalled upon throughout the entire experience (Darling-Hammond et al., 2017). The ideology behind professional learning activities is a stark contrast to the commonly held professional development seminars.

Professional development has been designed and popularized to be something of value to researchers, administrators, school leaders, and teachers (Cassidy et al., 2020). When practically constructed, professional development seminars are an opportunity to build new and veteran school employees into more effective and efficient team members (Darling-Hammond et al., 2017; Krasnoff, 2015). Appropriately administered professional development requires effectively modeled strategies to promote culture and expectations while explaining how ineffective systems negatively impact a program's mission and vision (Mizell, 2010). COVID-19 required and inspired various educational systems to adjust professional development where both traditional and non-traditional platforms supported a more individualized approach towards training opportunities (Reimers et al., 2020). This progressive shift away from training the group towards cultivating the individual is where professional development transforms into professional learning.

While professional development tends to aim for universal tactics that build the group's ability to meet predetermined benchmarks, professional learning emphasizes the value of an individual's agency (Calvert, 2016). The demarcation between professional development and professional learning processes is pertinent as lethargic approaches to professional development may evolve into unintended consequences that ultimately reinforce impractical and unproductive behaviors (Hicks et al., 2018; Wray et al., 2000; Cassidy et al., 2020). Professional learning activities are self-driven, motivating the individual to be more responsible for their professional practice and becoming mindful of both micro- and macro-level issues that may hinder themselves, their students, work colleagues, and community stakeholders (Scherff, 2018; Hicks et al., 2018).

Coming from a variety of educational backgrounds and employment dispositions, the authors build off the suggestions of Hicks et al., (2018) and "look at teacher growth from a learning perspective and recalibrate what teachers do to grow their practice as professional learning rather than professional development" (p. 3). Providing insight and forward-thinking, this book will examine dynamic educational topics that hopefully influences professional learning pedagogy, research, and practice with topics including reflective practices, content-area literacies, ESL/International students, providing writing feedback, instructional coaching, culturally responsive instruction, struggling readers, and parental/family engagement.

In Chapter 1, Michael Ladick reflects on an illogical attempt to develop a dissertation and how the lessons learned have impacted his identity as a researcher, educator, and professional learner. In Chapter 2, Crystal Dail Rose critically examines professional learning for mentor teachers and offers an alternative model where the cycles of collaborative action research are used to refine a contextualized professional development model supporting teacher capacity for mentoring preservice teachers in a school–university partnership.

In Chapter 3, Charity Embley investigates the need to traverse challenges stemming from opposition to equality and diversity conversations while describing the balance of providing critical cultural information from other ethnicities, protecting against stereotypes, and professional learning approaches to connect underlying multicultural education theories. In Chapter 4, Lindsay Malootian and Yvonne Cásares Khan offer practical literacy strategies that can unite families and classrooms to combat deficit thinking in various educational contexts and provide strategies to bond families and classrooms with literacy events.

In Chapter 5, Cesar Riojas focuses on professional learning techniques for English Language Learner in elementary and secondary education (K-12) while exploring various multi-modal literacy professional learning strategies to help educators develop activities to create a digitally cultured environment where all students can feel connected. In Chapter 6, Shona Rose investigates the characteristics, and the resulting student impact, of teachers who employ the stance of collaborator as opposed to a corrector to provide insight into processes for evaluating student products and decisions that lead to planning, selecting, and delivering feedback.

In Chapter 7, Elizabeth Davis Jones assists to re-conceptualize literacy instruction by providing various perspectives and practices to empower educators by providing critical literacy instruction in new learning spaces with pathways for providing diverse opportunities for digital literacy and citizenship. Finally, in Chapter 8, Rachel Herny, Chad Knesek, and Emily Hill Ottinger explore what professional development versus professional learning means at different schooling stages for content-area literacies in a 21st-century educational environment by refining the current understanding of content literacy skills and knowledge by exploring content-area literacy from elementary, middle, and the secondary levels.

References

Calvert, L. (2016). *Moving from compliance to agency: What teachers need to make professional learning work.* Oxford, OH: Learning Forward and NCTAF. Retrieved December 9, 2020, from https://learningforward.org/wp-content/uploads/2017/08/moving-from-compliance-to-agency.pdf

Cassidy, J., Ortlieb, E., & Grote-Garcia, S. (2020). What's Hot in Literacy: New Topics and New Frontiers are Abuzz. *Literacy Research and Instruction*, 1-12.

Darling-Hammond, L., Hyler, M. E., & Gardner, M. (2017). *Effective teacher professional development.* Retrieved December 2, 2020 from https://static1.squarespace.com/static/56b90cb101dbae64ff707585/t/5ade348e-70a6ad624d417339/1524511888739/NO_LIF~1.PDF

Hicks, T., & Sailors, M. (2018). Democratizing professional growth with teachers: From development to learning

Preface

[Literacy leadership brief]. Newark. *DE: International Literacy Association.*

Krasnoff, B. (2015). What the Research Says about Class Size, Professional Development, and Recruitment, Induction, and Retention of Highly Qualified Teachers: A Compendium of the Evidence on Title II, Part A, Program-Funded Strategies. *Northwest Comprehensive Center.*

Mizell, H. (2010). *Why Professional Development Matters.* Learning Forward. 504 South Locust Street, Oxford, OH 45056.

Reimers, F., Schleicher, A., Saavedra, J., & Tuominen, S. (2020). Supporting the continuation of teaching and learning during the COVID-19 Pandemic. *OECD, 1*(1), 1-38.

Scherff, L. (2018). Distinguishing professional learning from professional development. *Regional Educational Laboratory.* Retrieved December 9, 2020 from https://ies.ed.gov/ncee/edlabs/regions/pacific/blogs/blog2_DistinguishingProfLearning.asp#:~:text=Professional%20development%2C%20which%20%E2%80%9Chappens%20to,and%20customized%20to%20teachers'%20needs

Wray, D., & Medwell, J. (2000). Professional Development for Literacy Teaching: the evidence from effective teachers. *Journal of In-Service Education, 26*(3), 487-498.

Foreword

Mellinee Lesley, Texas Tech University

In 1998, during the early years of the national standards movement, I began my career in higher education with a study that examined the tenuous role of teachers' knowledge in a professional development initiative I was leading. As part of this inquiry, I explored the omnipresent element of external authority that guided the ways teachers were asked to frame their thinking. Little did I know the impact state and national standards would play in much of the credentialing and curricular efforts of educators in the ensuing years. Since 1998, I have continued to provide professional development at numerous schools. Sometimes these initiatives were one-day events. Sometimes, like my dissertation study, they involved graduate course credit and lasted the length of a school year. Sometimes they involved other external partners like the National Writing Project or the National Institute for Excellence in Teaching. I have taught at a Professional Development School and participated in more professional learning community meetings than I can count. In the last five years, my work in professional development has been driven by engaged scholarship with the goals of shared decision-making, leading to the co-construction of new knowledge. In all of these contexts, however, professional learning has been riddled with norms and expectations that rarely attend to the unique experiences and insights of the individual.

Reading *Purposeful Development of Professional Learning Processes* brought me to the beginning of my career as a teacher educator and academic as the authors of this book raise similar questions to the ones I examined in 1998. Even though the field of education is confronted with new social and curricular dilemmas in 2022, professional development in K-12 and post-secondary settings have long occupied a contested space where inequity pulls at the seams of every interaction. This book addresses such tensions by interrogating the multiplicity of ways professional learning occurs as the authors examine their experiences with culturally responsive pedagogy, content area and disciplinary literacies, multilingualism, English learners, border pedagogies, blended learning, effective feedback, cosmopolitan critical literacy, and digital literacies. Collectively, the authors take the position that meaningful professional development is individualized, attentive to cultural nuances, grounded in logical applications, and propelled by personal accountability. By exploring moments of intellectual departure in various educational contexts, the authors distinguish between professional development driven by hegemonic agendas and professional learning driven by reflexive inquiry. The chapters move between personal accounts and pragmatic recommendations in ways that call into question assumptions about meaningful professional learning and invite the reader to consider the pitfalls of arbitrary and deficit thinking. For instance, Rose (Chapter 2) ponders the extent to which K-12 mentor teachers should collaborate in the design of their professional learning. Similarly, Malootian and Khan (Chapter 4) argue families should play a greater role as stakeholders in professional teacher learning. All of the chapters examine how knowledge is constructed in educational settings for students and teachers as the authors interrogate their practice and ways of knowing.

This volume offers a weaving together of personal narratives, recommendations for teaching, and observations about how to cultivate authentic professional learning. Thus, the chapters initiate a dialogue about the importance of stance, place, technology, and lived experience in shaping knowledge. Professional learning is a continual and sometimes elusive process. Examining the ways adults come to understand their craft as educators and researchers reminds us that learning is a personal journey.

Chapter 1

The Professional Learnings of an Arrogant Neophyte

Michael Ladick, Ph.D.

Abstract

Reflection provides an opportunity to revisit a lot of undesirable learning curves and unforeseen obstacles. Reflecting can be inspired from a variety of affairs including a desire to seek clarity about inept experiences to calibrate pending or future circumstances that garner professional direction, awareness, and growth. In this chapter, Michael Ladick provides a candid reflection about the steps and processes that ultimately led to a failed dissertation and ends by encouraging professional learners a pathway away from maladroitness and instead towards redemption, solace, and progress.

Introduction

Reflection is a powerful professional learning tool. Reflecting on past experiences is a willful way to connect, or reconnect with, knowledge about past perspectives, successes, failures, decisions, or outcomes (Biesta & Burbules 2003; Dewey, 1997; Šarić & Šteh, 2017). "Reflection is turning a topic over in various aspects and in various lights so that nothing significant about it shall be overlooked" (Dewey, 1997, p. 57). Regularly reflecting on previous practices can be a professionally nonintrusive form of checks and balances, helping to avoid the creation of echo chambers where explicit and implicit biases may reside (Maxcy, 1991). Because any "experience is deepened and enriched by intelligent reflection" (Quirk, 2003, p. 7), these reflective critiques of the self can be necessary and valuable exercises that help mitigate, and navigate, speculative minefields.

While potentially sensitive, reflection should not be a stringent process and instead one that simply and clearly explicates events that led up to an experience and the insights that followed (Dewey, 1938; Tanner & Tanner, 2007). As complex as the stories may be, the reflective process simply requires a struggle, location, suggested solution(s), the rationale for set suggestions, and acceptance or rejection of what happened (Dewey, 1997). Throughout the reflective process, the "constant and complex interchange between subjective feeling and objective demonstration" (Maddux & Donnett, 2015, p. 72) should be elaborated upon with a simplistic and transparent goal: to improve our current state by telling the truth.

When executed in good conscience, reflections can positively influence professional agency, helping parse the interconnected versus detached dichotomy of an experience providing keen, applicable context to situations (Anfara et al., 2002; Šarić & Šteh, 2017). Conceptually, the value of reflection is not solely based on what is or is not known within a specific moment. Instead, reflection relies on an individual's ability to recognize there was a series of events that progressed throughout an experience and, when recalled upon, can provide useful information when similar situations present themselves and reasonable methods for resolution when necessary (Addams, 1902; Biesta & Burbules, 2003; Calvert, 2016). Taking into consideration that until the time comes we do not know what we do not know, I certainly have a humbling story to tell.

The Disastrous Dissertation

I always wanted to go for my doctorate and after eight years of teaching, I decided to go for a Ph.D. in curriculum and instruction. While keeping my full-time job, I happily navigated the hybrid classroom environment with many late nights writing and researching since it was something I enjoyed and wanted to do. As the son of two teachers, it always felt very natural to be a student of learning and learning processes. Although my two-and-a-half years of classwork had plenty of challenges, I quietly struggled to transition from doctoral student to independent researcher upon entering the dissertation process. During the early stages of my research, I was intensely focused on fighting against the mechanisms that further produced and supported hidden agendas within the walls of financial education classrooms.

After reading Arthur's (2012) book, I was fascinated with how neoliberal ideology was seeping into financial literacy education, resources, and programs. Arthur emphasized how schools have a civic obligation to protect financial education programs "because the school is a site that is widely expected to create citizens who can renew and contribute to our democracy" (Arthur, 2012, p. 1). Invigorated by his discussion, and following my qualifying exams, I decided to focus on risk management and insurance standards and critically inquire how "connections which may be hidden from people, such as the connections between language, power and ideology" (Fairclough, 2001, p. 4), may exist within financial education curricula at both the national and state levels. Digging deeper into the risk management and insurance literature, it became clear how challenging the concepts were to comprehend and how a financial literacy educator, who may not be informed in this intricate area, may not question state and nationally recognized resources being produced and instead chose to simply recite the information provided. My newfound research mindset had me aggressively attentive towards some national policy shifts that I considered legitimate concerns to students and their financial well-being.

After the 2016 presidential election, the Trump administration rolled back the U.S. Department of Labor's stance on the fiduciary rule (Protess & Davis, 2017), dismantled the boards responsible for monitoring the financial watchdogs and consumer advocacy groups (Price & Schroeder, 2018), and rolled back Dodd–Frank regulations (Werner, 2018). As best I could interpret, these fiscal policy shifts were subtle yet serious changes that could impact students' current and future financial well-being. With policy decisions appearing to impact a variety of social, political and economic landscapes, it seemed reasonable to critically and frame about what was happening in financial education curricula.

Early into my investigation, I was convinced neoliberals would subvert their ideology in curricular aptitudes that parallels risk management strategies: risk management and insurance standards. Neoliberals support aggressive deregulation, privatization and globalization ideologies (Thorsen & Lie, 2006) and a predominant neoliberal doctrine that caught my attention was a subset of privatization: academic capitalism. Within an educational setting, the academic capitalists compel schools "to adopt commercial models of knowledge, skills, curriculum, finance, accounting, and management organization" (Levidow, 2007, p. 238). After examining the acknowledgement sections of national and state financial education curricula, the fingerprints of for-profit corporations, financial institutions, and insurance companies were all over these documents. With the understanding that there are limited markets for financial education curricula, it seemed reasonable to assert that the academic capitalists, wherever they may be hidden, would build standards around their "selfish maximization of their own profits and consumers' selfish maximization of their own preferences" (Wolff & Resnick, 2012, p. 103). However, I came to find out that these particular sentiments were not necessarily neoliberal so much as they were neoclassical.

A neoclassical framework, economically speaking, presumes consumers as having needs, prioritizing them, and making choices to maximize satisfaction (Zalega, 2014). In an effort to capitalize on utility, the consumer will select specific goods and services via preferences, and the awareness of these preferences has the consumer acting in various markets under the assumption these decisions are made rationally (Arnsperger & Varoufakis, 2006; Keita, 2012). Essentially, the corporatist enterprises that produce goods, services, or expertise have an incredible amount of influence over consumers as they make choices under the assumption they are fair and equal counterparts when, in reality, consumers are exposed to a limited number of options and opportunities.

After six months of attempting to build a content analysis that melded risk management, insurance, financial risk, and neoclassical codes to observe whether or not risk management and insurance standards were tarnished, the plug was rightfully pulled by my dissertation chair. I remember, with vivid detail exactly where I was at when I received the email telling me how my dissertation needed such severe revisions that it had to be put on hold and continually thank my wife for talking me out of buying plane tickets to fly down to campus while in complete ire. For months, I thought I was preparing to fight the neoclassical regime destined to dominate the soul of the student as a new, fresh breed of the consumer, while instead, I generated a document that was downright tragic.

An Open-Minded Observation: The Critical Issue Was Me

My attitude throughout writing the first dissertation iteration held that it was not my fault if someone who reads the document does not understand what I have written. That outlook could not have been more conceited and wrong. I had no business being so wrapped up in trying to find something, anything, related to the financial literacy-critical-financial risk-risk management and insurance-neoclassical paradigm I attempted to concoct. Instead, I should have become aware of how forced the research was and why the thesis, as a whole, was overzealous. Even now, taking the time to reread the document is a painful experience as everything that sounded and appeared logical feels artificial and counterproductive. The dissertation's demise was no one's fault but my own. Simply put, I produced an overly manufactured and illogical disaster of a dissertation that, upon further review, was deemed unsatisfactory. So be it, and thank goodness.

While there is a happy ending to this story, I defended and graduated the following spring, the salient point moving forward is not that I turned a tragedy into an accomplishment, but how and why this experience impacts my professional roles and responsibilities. Although the story has not changed, my perspective on the events that unfolded certainly have evolved. Taking the time to write it all down and compartmentalize each step within the experience has provided me with growth from several different agentic standpoints.

First, as a now 14-year educator, I have always treated reflection as an abstract practice instead of a systematic opportunity to professionally learn by pausing, understanding different positions, and examining professional miscalculations. To become better educated on professional indiscretions, one has to be willing to connect and learn from past experiences through transparent and cognizant considerations (Addams, 1909). I can admit how much of a challenge it is to patiently describe situations in a nonreactive manner because personal feelings can present themselves quickly in professional environments. Integrating reflection into my teaching practice has helped mitigate professional lapses and made me more aware of others within agile situations as they unfold.

Second, as an independent education researcher, I have learned how to embrace imperfection and dissect niche processes. The fact is when writing my first dissertation iteration, inexperience exposed my

5

inability to construct an argument that concisely connected theoretical relationships, described conceptual categories, and demonstrated concise methodological steps. Critical inquiry requires acute attention to detail, and I was neither keen nor attentive. Was I obsessive in my attempt to conduct a critical inquiry? Yes. Can most problems in the education field be framed as critical issues? Sure, with enough effort. Should those in the field of education have critical tunnel vision? No. The use of critical inquiry to generalize an individual, or groups of individuals, as having malicious, systematized, or power-driven intent is careless. Doing so diminishes the power of critical perspectives and could embolden those who do not embrace its ideological premise.

Finally, as a professional learner, I have come to appreciate how professional learning is a process that requires reflection and warrants the investigation of some dreadful past perspectives and affairs. This is especially true when trying to decipher the difference between looking for trouble and finding something troublesome (Badley, 2003; Shalin, 1992). Rationalizing this experience from a professional learning perspective, it is reasonable to recognize how anyone reading my prior work would struggle to delineate between deeming me innocently negligent versus purposely manipulative. The former seems relatively harmless and lacks the manifestation of deliberately deceitful actions because of a virtuous sense of diligence. The latter tends to undermine the opportunity for inoffensive thought because of a defiant attitude rejecting available information. Regardless, both options are undesirable and unappealing positions for a professional learner to acquiesce and should be avoided at all costs.

Closing Thoughts

This reflective chapter was rewritten and repackaged after I received a comment from a journal reviewer who rejected the first article I ever submitted. The failed journal submission, with a very similar outline to this chapter, came back with one salient critique about me: that I had *the overconfidence of an arrogant neophyte*. They were not lying. Though, while the reviewer's commentary made me wholeheartedly rethink the depths to which I should describe my experience, I would recommend to anyone looking to incorporate reflection as a part of their professional learning practice to be sure that the process not be done in bad faith. For example, the reviewer did not tell me I needed to reflect but that I needed *to integrate more personally relevant in-formation*. Fair point.

Thus, while my first attempts at a dissertation and journal article were somewhat idiosyncratic and could have been perceived as presumptuous, it was ultimately my decision to honestly reflect on the entire experience. I would never let someone, anyone, recommend reflection to me as part of some self-righteous, virtue-signaling standpoint to didactically ascertain an unfounded opinion or overshadowing of my competence, abilities, or intent. Neither should you. Reflection should be a moment of enlightenment, not infringement. Issues or apprehensions within our immediate educational realm should not be the ones we create or others make us believe exist. So embrace your arrogant inner neophyte and revel in your professional journey whilst finding liberation and gusto about all of your educational experiences no matter the conclusion. I know I did.

References

Addams, J. (1902). *Democracy and Social Ethics.* The Macmillan Co.

Addams, J. (1909). *The spirit of youth and the city streets (Vol. 80).* University of Illinois Press.

Anfara Jr, V. A., Brown, K. M., & Mangione, T. L. (2002). Qualitative analysis on stage: Making the research process more public. *Educational researcher, 31*(7), 28-38.

Arnsperger, C. and Varoufakis, Y. (2006). What Is Neoclassical Economics? The three axioms responsible for its theoretical oeuvre, practical irrelevance and, thus, discursive power. *Panoeconomicus, 53*(1), 5-18.

Arthur, C. (2012). *Financial literacy education: Neoliberalism, the Consumer and the Citizen.* Sense Publishers.

Badley, G. (2003). The crisis in educational research: a pragmatic approach. *European educational research journal, 2*(2), 296-308.

Biesta, G.J., and Burbules, N.C., *Pragmatism and educational research.* Rowman and Littlefield Publishers Inc.

Calvert, L. (2016). Moving from compliance to agency: What teachers need to make professional learning work. Oxford, OH: Learning Forward and NCTAF. Retrieved December 9, 2020 from https://learningforward.org/wp-content/uploads/2017/08/moving-from-compliance-to-agency.pdf

Dewey, J. (1938). 1997. *Experience and education.* First Touchstone.

Dewey, J. (1997). *How we think.* Dover Publications, Inc.

Fairclough, N. (2001). *Language and power.* Pearson Education.

Keita, L. (2012). Revealed Preference Theory, Rationality, and Neoclassical economics: science or ideology. *Africa Development, 37*(4), 73-116.

Levidow, L. (2007). Marketizing Higher Education: Neoliberal Strategies and Counterstrategies. In Ross, E. W., & Gibson, R. J. (Eds.). *Neoliberalism and education reform.* Hampton Press.

Maddux, H. C. and Donnett, D. (2015). John Dewey's Pragmatism: Implications for Reflection in Service-Learning. *Michigan Journal of Community Service Learning* Vol. 21, no. 2: 64-73. Retrieved from *https://eric.ed.gov/?id=EJ1116448*

Maxcy, S.J. (1991). *Educational Leadership: A Critical Pragmatic Perspective. Critical Studies in Education and Culture Series.* Greenwood Publishing Group, Inc.

Price, M. and Schroeder, P. (2018) *Trump-appointed consumer watchdog director just fired the agency's entire advisory board after criticism of his leadership.* Business Insider. http://www.businessinsider.com/mick-mulvaney-cfpb-director-fires-agencys-advisory-board-after-criticism-2018-6

Protess, B. and Davis, J.H., (2017) *Trump Moves to Roll Back Obama-Era Financial Regulations.* New York Times. https://www.nytimes.com/2017/02/03/business/dealbook/trump-congress-financial-regulations.html

Quirk, M. J. (2003). Dewey's version of pragmatism. Molloy College: Philosophy Department, Sophia Project.

Retrieved from http://www.sophia-project.org/uploads/1/3/9/5/13955288/quirk_dewey1.pdf

Šarić, M., & Šteh, B. (2017). Critical reflection in the professional development of teachers: Challenges and possibilities. *CEPS journal*, *7*(3), 67-85.

Shalin, D. N. (1992). Critical theory and the pragmatist challenge. *American Journal of Sociology*, *98*(2), 237-279.

Tanner, D., & Tanner, L. N. (2007). *Curriculum development: Theory into practice*. Pearson Education.

Thorsen, D. E., & Lie, A. (2006). What is neoliberalism. *Oslo, University of Oslo, Department of Political Science, Manuscript*, 1-21.

Werner, E. (2018) *Trump signs law rolling back post-financial crisis banking rules*. Washington Post. https://www.washingtonpost.com/business/economy/trump-signs-law-rolling-back-post-financial-crisis-banking-rules/2018/05/24/077e3aa8-5f6c-11e8-a4a4-c070ef53f315_story.html

Wolff, R. D., and Resnick, S. A. (2012). *Contending economic theories: neoclassical, Keynesian, and Marxian*. MIT Press.

Zalega, T. (2014). Consumer and Consumer Behaviour in the Neoclassical and Behavioural Economic Approach. *Konsumpcja i rozwoj*, *4*(9), 64-79.

Chapter 2

A Critical Examination and Challenge Regarding Professional Learning for Cooperating Teachers with the Cycles of Collaborative Action Research

Crystal Dail Rose, Ph.D., Tarleton State University

Abstract

Teacher educators are often charged with providing professional learning for cooperating teachers (i.e., lead teachers, mentor teachers) working in partnering schools that host their preservice teachers. Although literature challenges top-down models of professional learning, university–school partnerships, for professional development for mentor teachers typically do not follow a model that allows for collaborative inquiry. This chapter critically examines professional learning for cooperating teachers by giving a brief overview of professional learning for cooperating teachers, a discussion of action research as professional development, a description of one university's experience, and offers an alternative model using the cycles of collaborative action research to refine a contextualized professional development model designed to support teacher capacity for mentoring preservice teachers in a school–university partnership.

Introduction

Teacher educators are often charged with providing professional learning for cooperating teachers (i.e., lead teachers, mentor teachers) working in partnering schools that host their preservice teachers. This professional learning typically involves presentations by experts that are conducted in short sessions at various intervals throughout the school year (Burke et al., 2010). Literature challenges top-down models of professional learning (Darling-Hammond, 2005) and calls for a more contemporary view of mentoring-a "social practice" and "cooperative human activity" (Kemmis et al., 2014, p. 155) where mentors share power for the "purpose of empowerment" (Fletcher, 2012, p. 69). University–school partnerships for professional development for mentor teachers typically do not follow a model that allows for collaborative inquiry. In fact, "there is no universally accepted set of supports that constitutes a good, supportive early training and ongoing professional development system..." (García & Weiss, 2019, p. 6). This chapter critically examines professional learning for cooperating teachers by giving a brief overview of professional learning for cooperating teachers, a discussion of action research as professional development, a description of one university's experience, and offers an alternative model using the cycles of collaborative action research to refine a contextualized professional development model designed to support teacher capacity for mentoring preservice teachers in a school–university partnership.

Professional Learning for Teachers

Since 2015, when former President Obama reauthorized the 1965 *Elementary and Secondary Education Act* as the *Every Student Succeeds Act* (ESSA, 2015), professional development for teachers has been a common thread of discussion among state, district, campus, school, and classroom leaders. The ESSA replaced No Child Left Behind (NCLB, 2001) and intended to shift the way school success is defined and supported. Furthermore, the ESSA allowed states to allocate funding toward professional development geared toward improving instructional strategies of teachers, principals, or other school leaders (PUBLIC LAW, 2015).

In addition to federal and state requirements for professional development for teachers, researchers find a plethora of reasons why good, high-quality, continuous professional development is proven to improve teacher practices and student outcomes. Existing research provides evidence for many reasons professional development should be at the forefront of our thinking, especially in regards to improvements to teacher practices, student outcomes, and teacher retention (i.e., García & Weiss, 2019; Akiba & Liang, 2016; Didion, et al., 2020; Gesel, et al., 2021; Sims & Fletcher-Wood, 2021; Bill & Melinda Gates Foundation, 2014; Darling-Hammond, Burns, et al. 2017; Darling-Hammond, Hyler, et al. 2017; ESSA, 2015; Hill, 2009; Ingersoll & Collins, 2018; Jensen, et al. 2016; Kraft, et al., 2018; Mizell, 2010). Although the need is present, offering the high-quality professional development required by ESSA and described in research has not come without challenges to districts. In fact, some believe evidence-based policies such as No Child Left Behind and ESSA have been largely ineffective (Cavendish, et al., 2021). There is limited access to the types of professional development that are "highly valued" and proven "more effective" (García & Weiss, 2019, p. 1). For the most part, "novice and veteran teachers largely don't get the time and resources they need to study, reflect, and prepare their practice" (García & Weiss, 2019, p. 1). In addition, teachers are not satisfied with their professional development experiences, are not immersed in a learning community, and have little access to a mentor or useful professional development (García & Weiss, 2019).

Current Literature Recommendations for Teacher Professional Development

Recently, there have been a number of studies pointing toward specific components needed in teacher professional development. Specifically, PD should include supports to strengthen teachers' opportunities for advancement rather than "just survival" (García & Weiss, 2020, p. 7). Sancar and colleagues (2021) put forth a new framework for understanding teachers' professional development. They determined the need for a "holistic approach that arises, reviews, and interprets all components of the process" in order to better understand how to design "effective, efficient, inclusive, and continuous" professional development PD process for teachers" (p. 8). Based on an examination of current literature, they determined PD should carefully consider teacher characteristics and their own individual strengths and concerns within their actual context. When teachers feel the PD values their own individual characteristics, their motivation and enthusiasm may increase. Sancar et al. (2021) call for more emphasis on the context, environment, a common vision, and collaboration.

Cavendish and colleagues (2021) build on these ideas with the notion of creating professional development that is "teacher responsive" according to the teachers' own identified strengths and needs (p. 318). Professional development should be continuous, supportive, collaborative, growth-oriented, context-sensitive, and build collective responsibility by teachers. It should include collaborative decision-making, collective construction of effective practice, fit the needs of teachers' identity, and provide numerous opportunities for teachers to collaborate and contribute to the actual design of their own professional learning.

Since the authorization of ESSA in 2015, there has been an abundance of research available for states, districts, and schools around the content and impact of professional learning for teachers, in addition to what is described in the section above. In addition, there is a wealth of literature delineating the importance of cooperating or mentoring teachers on the effectiveness of preservice or novice teachers (i.e., Matsko, et al., 2020), as well as the learning that occurs on the part of the cooperating or mentor teacher due to the mentoring relationship and tasks therein (i.e., Smith & Nadelson, 2016). The recommendations for professional development specifically to support teachers who are mentoring preservice teachers are not as prevalent.

Current Literature Recommendations for Cooperating Teacher Professional Development

In 2010, state and federal policymakers, along with the National Council for Accreditation of Teacher Education called for a transformation of teacher preparation through intensive practice in school-based settings (National Council for Accreditation of Teacher Education, 2010). This recommendation brought an increase in the amount of time preservice teachers spent in the field with a mentor or cooperating teacher. As Clarke and colleagues put it, mentors play "one of the most critical roles in preservice teacher education" (Clarke et al., 2012, p. 167).

Although literature calls for more collaboration where mentors share power (Kemmis et al., 2014; Fletcher, 2012), university–school partnerships for professional development for mentor teachers typically do not follow a model that allows for collaboration, especially concerning design. This idea of the transformation of professional development for mentors is not a new one. In fact, Cochran-Smith and Lytle called for this transformation since the early 1990s and 2000s, especially concerning teacher education for justice and equity (see Cochran-Smith, 1991a, 1991b, 2001a, 2001b, 2001c; Cochran-Smith & Lytle, 1999, 2009). In a recent article, Cochran-Smith

(2020) describes several premises regarding teaching and learning. One of which is based on her work in 1995: "knowledge is socially constructed and fluid, and all participants in teacher education, including teacher candidates, university instructors and supervisors, classroom teachers, and students, are knowers, active agents in their own constructions of meaning, and, always, learners" (Cochran-Smith, 2020, p. 51). Cochran-Smith (2020) and others call for a transformed model for teacher professional development to include discussions, reflections on specific teaching and learning approaches, teacher-centered collaboration, and teacher-driven research-based learning that is context-specific and teacher knowledge is valued (see also Akiba & Liang, 2016; Cavendish et al., 2021; García & Weiss, 2020; Sancar et al., 2021). The one-size-fits-all delivery model for teachers is outdated. Teachers' professional development is essential, yet, most of the packaged professional development programs for teachers are not successful and have little influence (Wei, et al., 2010; Yigit & Bagceci, 2017). The professional development needs of teachers in an ever-changing, highly variable, educational landscape are not being met. Action Research as professional development could remedy this need.

Cycles of Action Research as Professional Development

Introduction to Action Research

Lewin (1946) described action research as a spiral of steps where one plans, acts, observes, then evaluates the result of the action. Carr and Kemmis (1983) define the action research process involving cycles of self-critical and reflective processes where teachers learn about their classroom environments and teaching practices. It was designed as a way for people to learn from their own experience. In 1974, an important shift occurred as teachers involved in the Language and Learning Project in Australia looked at their own pedagogical practices and documented their reflections on classroom learning. Teachers were the "investigating agents," and, for the first time, many of the teachers "engaged in the production of their own knowledge" (Grundy, 1997, p. 129). The research is specifically personally constructed by the practitioner within the social context in which he or she lives and learns (Wenger, 1998). Another key piece of the action research process is the knowledge and understanding built along the way within the particular context in a way that teachers are able to change their thinking and practice (Somekh, 1993). This power to bring about change in knowledge and understanding among teachers and from teachers is of key importance for quality in action research (Capobianco & Feldman, 2006).

Action Research as Customized Professional Development

Classroom-based action research, with the investigation of the teaching and learning within the actual, real context of the classroom, is not only viable, but a more meaningful and valuable alternative. When teachers are able to develop their own goals, action research can be used to personalize their professional development. Teachers investigate and improve their own practice within their own classrooms, therefore, the learning and growth are more meaningful (Mertler, 2013). The most useful professional development focuses on active teaching, assessment, observation, and reflection (Darling-Hammond & McLaughlin, 1995; Desimone & Stuckey, 2014; Mizell, 2010). Well-designed professional development could improve both teaching practices and student achievement (Wei et al., 2010). In addition, professional development mentoring sessions should be social, cooperative, empowering, collaborative, embedded, contextual, reflective, supportive; yet, this approach is uncommon in the field of teacher education (Kemmis et al., 2014; Fletcher, 2012; Romijn et al., 2021). There are multiple models for action research in the classroom; however, the sections below highlight an approach found in literature shown to work effectively in district–university partnerships, collaborative action research.

Collaborative Action Research

A critique of action research in the 1990s pointed out the majority of studies include an outsider (an external researcher or facilitator) joining a group of in-service teachers to assist them in reflecting on their practice in order to make improvements, thus, action research is not a "natural process" because it requires teachers to be "systematic, collaborative, and critical" (Johnston, 1994). Feldman (1998) remedied this critique with less reliance on university operations and described the notion of collaborative action research as a normal practice with conversation, knowledge, and understanding within the particular context and situation. Feldman's model of collaborative action research acknowledges collaborative, sustained conversation as a form of research. The participants in this conversation move between the conversation itself, their "immediate understanding," and a "global understanding" where the "conversation leads to a new understanding and the new understanding shapes the conversation" (Feldman, 1998, p. 36).

Collaborative action research, where teachers come together to solve problems of practice, make changes and improvements, and focus on their own professional development in a direction they most need, meets the call for a more contemporary approach to professional learning and is a viable alternative to professional development programs that are not useful (Yigit & Bagceci, 2017). Specifically, in order to fully understand this model, we must examine the goals of collaborative action research, effective partnerships between researchers and schools, and the challenges and successes that come with this work.

Feldman (1998) identifies the goals of action research as "the improvement of practice and an improved understanding of the educational situation in which the practice is immersed" (p. 28). Collaborative action research is characterized by four key ideas: teachers working as a team; the focus is on a common issue, problem, or goal; teachers have a synergy that inspires one another; the focus is on creating momentum, insight, learning, and growth around the issue under investigation (Clauset, et al., 2008). Mertler (2013) takes these goals a step further with the idea that teachers set the action research goals for themselves, then they are held accountable for what they discover through a systematic process of data collection and reflection. This would empower teachers to invest ownership in their own teacher evaluation process. Riel (2019) names three goals of collaborative action research: to improve professional practice through continual learning and progressive problem solving; to achieve a deeper understanding of organizational change through collective actions; to improve the community in which one's practice is embedded through participatory action learning or research (p. 3).

The process of collaborative action research is flexible and can be customized to meet the needs of the teachers involved (Yigit & Bagceci, 2017). In fact, each action researcher has flexibility within his or her own approach as the context and support structures vary (Riel, 2019). A number of various action research cycles can be found in the literature (see Feldman, 1996; Mertler, 2012, 2013; Yigit & Bagceci, 2017; Riel, 2019; Riel & Rowell, 2016); however, effective partnerships are necessary for this high level of collaboration.

A Critical Examination of Partnerships Utilizing Collaborative Action Research as Professional Development between Universities and Schools: Purposes, Challenges, and Successes

Several have successfully built effective partnerships between researchers and schools using the collaborative action research model with preservice teachers (i.e., Saribas & Akdemir, 2020; Bilican et al., 2021; Aras, 2021), in-service teachers (i.e., Çayır & Yolcu, 2021; Aldridge et al., 2021), and veteran teachers (Buckley-Marudas, et al., 2021); however, since universities are typically charged with providing professional development to cooperating teachers (also known as mentor teachers, in-service teachers) who mentor their teacher residents (also known as student teachers, preservice teachers), the focus here is on universities who have utilized collaborative action research jointly with cooperating teachers and teacher residents in a way that builds an effective partnership with the purpose of improving their own practice.

Using Harzing's (2007) tool, Publish or Perish, the author conducted a critical examination of the top-cited literature in the field between 2015 and 2021. The purpose of this critical examination was to gain an understanding of whether or not universities and districts follow methodological recommendations found in current research, including informal discussions, data and critical reflections, collaboration, and teacher-driven research-based learning to build knowledge, inform theory, and change practice. Even more specifically, the author hoped to determine the purpose, challenges, and successes of collaborative action research partnerships between universities and schools that host preservice teachers since ESSA. There were only seven studies that met the methodological recommendations found in current research (see Parker et al., 2016; Shanks, 2016; Reagan, et al., 2017; Wolkenhauer & Hooser, 2021; Schulte & Klipfel, 2016; Garin & Harper, 2016; Rogers, 2017). The purpose described in these studies was to utilize action research with cooperating teachers and/ or teacher candidates in order to support their professional development. Some of the challenges were around contextual problems, such as navigating the cooperating teacher relationship. There were many successes, but the rich learning that occurs around using action research to improve his or her practice was listed in every study.

Although there are hundreds of empirical studies about the benefits of yearlong residencies, co-teaching, a collaboration between the university and the district, and using data to inform instruction, there are very few university-district partners who are actually engaging in action research. This critical examination did not yield many results describing the work of universities and districts engaging in methodological recommendations found in current research; however, the findings are useful nonetheless in determining next steps. In fact, many universities and schools understand the value in engaging in action research based on the recommendations in literature and aspire to partner with schools in this way; however, navigating the structures of the partnership and planning to engage in this high level of work takes time (see Burroughs et al. 2020). As Mertler (2013) suggests, engaging in collaborative action research as professional development requires a shift in mindset. Additionally, "Collaborative action research as a model of professional development requires both groups to navigate unfamiliar territory and redefine traditionally assumed roles" (West, 2011, p. 93-94). Although there are challenges involved in this work, a strong foundation and partnership such as those described in the next few sections at Tarleton State University seem to be a necessary first step. After describing the background of Tarleton's transformation, the author outlines Tarleton's experience of providing professional development to Cooperating Teachers, engaging in Action Research with Teacher Residents, then offers next steps for universities involved in effective partnerships with districts hosting their Teacher Residents.

Tarleton State University's Experience

Background

In 2019, Tarleton State underwent a rigorous application, interview, and selection process in order to apply for an innovative partnership with the University-School Partnerships for the Renewal of Educator Preparation (US PREP), a model born out of the work from Texas Tech University, in order to begin programmatic transformation and join the ranks of twelve other universities who were already renewing their own teacher preparation programs (US PREP, 2020). US PREP took what is known from research about the most impactful aspects of teacher preparation and built a model for universities to emulate. The five key attributes that researchers have found to be most impactful on teacher preparedness are:

- A focus on practice
- Mentoring and coaching
- A coherent vision of teaching
- Integration of coursework and clinical experiences
- Partnerships as the driving force for change and improvement

The author, Dr. Rose, first began her involvement in a contextualized professional development model in the fall of 2020 when she became a Site Coordinator for Tarleton State University during their first year of transformation with US PREP. With the US PREP model, the Tarleton teacher residents work in partner districts alongside cooperating teachers who are experienced and intentionally selected. Teacher Residents co-teach with their cooperating teacher for an entire school year. They are able to see, experience, practice, and refine their skills as an effective educator. This high-quality clinical experience with a full year of practice under an experienced, highly effective cooperating teacher propels Tarleton Teachers to truly be ready, day one of their teaching career, to teach all students.

A Collaborative, On-going, Contextualized Professional Development Model

Part of the responsibility of Site Coordinator is to offer monthly professional development training in order to prepare and support cooperating teachers. As described in prior sections of this chapter, literature points toward professional development that is collaborative and contextual (Sancar et al., 2021). In other words, the teachers, themselves need to see that the professional development actually applies to them, with their own individual characteristics, within their own classroom of students at that time and be able to take new learning and apply it that afternoon in their classrooms. Additionally, professional development needs to be continuous with collaborative decision making and to provide opportunities for teachers to contribute to the actual design of their professional learning (see also Petrie & McGee, 2012; Sharkey, et al., 2016; Fullan et al.,2015; Milner & Laughter, 2015; Diaz-Maggioli, 2004; Gabriel et al. 2011; Joubert & Sutherland, 2008; Darling-Hammond, Burns, et al. 2017). The US PREP model for professional development for cooperating teachers meets the criteria outlined in the literature.

The Tarleton teacher residents work in partner districts alongside cooperating teachers who are experienced and intentionally selected. The professional development is continuous and entails collaborative decision-making on the design of the sessions. Cooperating Teachers attend monthly professional development sessions in order to continue growing in their effectiveness for coaching their teacher residents. The professional development sessions are co-designed by the Site Coordinator and Cooperating Teachers according to the specific needs of Cooperating Teachers that month. At the end of each monthly session, Dr. Rose, with the support of her US PREP Site Coordinator Coach, Ms. Zavala, collected feedback from Cooperating Teachers about the usefulness of the session as well as areas of which they would like further support. The team used this feedback to plan the next session each month. This continuous feedback, where teachers share what they need and the university working to meet those needs, created an ongoing, collaborative, professional development design for the year that was unique to the specific context of the cooperating teachers in that district.

Action Research with Teacher Residents

In the US PREP design, Site Coordinators not only support the Cooperating Teachers in monthly professional development sessions, but they also often teach the courses taken by Teacher Residents, Teacher Residency I, and Teacher Residency II. In her work with US PREP designing these courses, Dr. Rose implemented an action-based research project titled, Student Perception Survey (SPS). This survey is transformative in teaching the Tarleton Teacher Residents to utilize student data to grow and improve their practice. The survey measures elements of the student experience that have been demonstrated to correlate most closely to student growth, including student learning, student-centered environment, classroom community, and classroom management. The survey was developed by the Colorado Legacy Foundation and included 34-items asking students about their learning experiences. There are two versions of the survey, grades 2-5 and grades 6-12. They set goals for their own practice based on proven instructional strategies for each SPS item based on the results Teacher Residents get from their students (Colorado Education Initiative, 2020). At the end of the year, they give the survey to their students again to measure their effectiveness in improving those specific areas. Although Tarleton is actively engaging both Cooperating Teachers and Teacher Residents, the author proposes the next steps for a collaborative, ongoing, contextualized professional development model, both for Tarleton and other universities involved in this high level of collaboration with partner districts, using collaborative action research with both Cooperating Teachers and Teacher Residents.

Next Steps: A Collaborative, On-going, Contextualized Professional Development Model with Action Research

Tarleton State University's partnership with US PREP and area districts has been transformational for all involved. Because of the continuous, ongoing feedback collected in the quarterly governance meetings, monthly cooperating teacher professional development sessions, and regularly from teacher residents about their day-to-day experiences, this work pushes all to use the data collected to be more effective in their own practice.

As described in the previous section, Tarleton State University currently supports Cooperating Teachers in professional development according to recommendations found in the literature. The professional development is collaborative, ongoing, and contextualized. Site Coordinators also engage in cycles of action research with their Teacher Residents in the Student Perception Survey project. Now, the challenge is to combine efforts with both Cooperating Teachers and Teacher Residents to provide collaborative, ongoing, and contextualized professional development that engages them in the cycles of action research. These next steps are not only relevant for Tarleton

~~State or universities working with US PREP, but for all universities~~ who have partnerships with districts that host their teacher residents.

Researchers describe the current partnerships between their university and district and communicate the desire to engage further in action research with their teacher residents and cooperating teachers (see Burroughs et al., 2020; Manzar-Abbas & Lu, 2015; Foy et al., 2018); however, according to the critical examination of the literature conducted and described earlier in the chapter, very few universities have the access, collaborative structure, and relationships in order to do this high-level work with districts (see Parker et al., 2016; Shanks, 2016; Reagan et al., 2017; Wolkenhauer & Hooser, 2021; Schulte & Klipfel, 2016; Garin & Harper, 2016; Rogers, 2017). Universities who have the access, collaborative structure, and relationships either due to their transformative work with US PREP or simply because of years of work developing partnerships could do this level of work with districts. For universities and districts that currently do not engage in a collaborative, ongoing, and contextualized partnership with cooperating teachers, this challenge would be more difficult to enact but something to work toward. The sections that follow describe a new, alternative model for professional development.

Action Research in the Cooperating Teacher–Teacher Resident Classroom

Tarleton State and other US PREP universities are just beginning to delve into a more contextualized, collaborative model for professional development with partner districts. Currently, Site Coordinators at Tarleton meet monthly with 90 cooperating teachers from partner districts who are participating in the yearlong Tarleton Teacher Residency Program. They use data from the field as well as from the Cooperating Teachers to design support that is specific to their needs at the time. Dr. Rose proposes an alternative model where they take this work a step further to support cooperating teacher capacity for mentoring our teacher residents in a school-university partnership in order to improve teacher quality and retention and student achievement engaging in action research. Cooperating Teachers and Teacher Residents will read an action research text to begin a discussion around the cycles of action research. As a team and with Site Coordinator support, they will collectively determine an area of focus for the action research study. They will use literature on action research, their classroom student achievement data, and contextual details about their classroom and teaching practices in order to determine a focus for the work and set specific dates to share their progress. This seminar will be the first stage of the action research cycle-planning. Throughout the semester, they will engage in the acting and reflecting/evaluating cycles of the project. In the following semester, they will come together for evaluation of data and determine further action (Lewin, 1946).

The conceptual framework for this work builds on the work of Romijn et al. (2021) to include the who, what, and how of the collaborative, ongoing, and contextualized professional development. As Mertler (2013) and others have determined, having educators engage in data-driven educational decision-making can be empowering, democratic, and participatory, resulting in richer, more meaningful learning for all involved. The "how" refers to the professional development strategies and delivery modes. For this work, the author and the Cooperating Teacher-Teacher Resident teams will rely on Riel's (2019) clarification of the collaborative nature of action research as a collaborative process WITH people in their own context in a way that builds understanding and change throughout the process. They will undergo action research as an iterative, cyclical process where one reflects on their practice, takes action, reflects on the action, then takes further action.

Conclusion

Romijn et al. (2021) agree with many other researchers that professional development for teachers should be embedded, contextual, reflective, and supportive; yet, "such an approach is still uncommon in the field of teacher preparation and support" (p. 97). Action research can help teachers "achieve transformative professional learning" (Lambirth et al., 2021, p. 829). Universities must build on the foundation of knowledge gained from researchers collaborating with teachers described throughout this chapter and deepen partnerships between universities and school districts in order to enact an alternative model for Cooperating Teacher Professional Development using the cycles of collaborative action research. This model could support teacher capacity for mentoring preservice teachers in order to effectively prepare the next generation of teachers. Those at Tarleton State, as well as others across the nation involved in this work, will enact this alternative model of professional development that is collaborative, ongoing, and contextualized in order to meet the needs of teachers and the students they serve.

References

Akiba, M., & Liang, G. (2016). Effects of teacher professional learning activities on student achievement growth. *The Journal of Educational Research, 109*, 99–110

Aldridge, J. M., Rijken, P. E., & Fraser, B. J. (2021). Improving learning environments through whole-school collaborative action research. *Learning Environments Research, 24*(2), 183-205.

Aras, S. (2021). Action research as an inquiry-based teaching practice model for teacher education programs. *Systemic Practice and Action Research, 34*, 153-168.

Bilican, K., Senler, B., & Karisan, D. (2021). Fostering teacher educators' professional development through collaborative action research. *International Journal of Progressive Education, 17*(2), 459-472.

Bill & Melinda Gates Foundation. (2014, December). *Teachers Know Best Teachers' Views on Professional Development*. U.S. Program. Retrieved November 27, 2021, from https://usprogram.gatesfoundation.org/-/media/dataimport/resources/pdf/2016/11/gates-pdmarketresearch-dec5.pdf

Buckley-Marudas, M. F. M., Dutton, J., Ellenbogen, C., Huang, G. H. C., & Schwab, S. (2021). Exploring veteran teachers' collaborative action research experiences through a school-university partnership: "Old dogs" try new tricks. *The Canadian Journal of Action Research, 22*(1), 45-68.

Burke, W., Marx, G. E., & Berry, J. E. (2010). Maintaining, reframing, and disrupting traditional expectations and outcomes for professional development with critical friends groups. *The Teacher Educator, 46*(1), 32–52.

Burroughs, G., Lewis, A., Battey, D., Curran, M., Hyland, N. E., & Ryan, S. (2020). From mediated fieldwork to co-constructed partnerships: A framework for guiding and reflecting on p-12 school–university partnerships. *Journal of Teacher Education, 71*(1), 122-134.

Capobianco, B. M., & Feldman, A. (2006). Promoting quality for teacher action research: Lessons learned from science teachers' action research. *Educational Action Research, 14*(4), 497-512.

Carr, W., & Kemmis, S. (1983). *Becoming critical: Knowing through action research*. Geelong: Deakin University.

Cavendish, W., Barrenechea, I., Young, A. F., Díaz, E., & Avalos, M. (2021). Urban teachers' perspectives of strengths and needs: The promise of teacher responsive professional development. *The Urban Review, 53*(2), 318-333.

Çayır, N. A., & Yolcu, A. (2021). A primary school teacher's journey on using drama method in the classroom: collaborative action research model. *International Journal of Progressive Education, 17*(5).

Clarke, A., Collins, J., Triggs, V., Nielsen, W., Augustine, A., Couter, D., Cunningham, J., Grigoriadis, T., Hardman, S., Hunter, L., Kinegal, J., Li, B., Mah, J., Mastin, K., Partridge, D., Pawer, L., Rasoda, S., Salbuvik, K., Ward, M., White, J. and Weil, F. (2012). The mentoring profile inventory: An online professional development resource for cooperating teachers. *Teaching Education, 23*(2), 167-194.

Clauset, K. H., Lick, D. W., & Murphy, C. U. (2008) *Schoolwide action research for professional learning communities: Improving student learning through the whole-faculty study groups approach*. Thousand Oaks, CA: Corwin.

Cochran-Smith, M. (2020). Teacher education for justice and equity: 40 years of advocacy. *Action in Teacher Education, 42*(1), 49-59.

Cochran-Smith, M. (1991a). Learning to teach against the grain. *Harvard Educational Review, 61*(3), 279–311.

Cochran-Smith, M. (1991b). Reinventing student teaching. *Journal of Teacher Education, 41*(2), 104–118.

Cochran-Smith, M. (2001a). Higher standards for prospective teachers: What's missing from the discourse? *Journal of Teacher Education, 52*(3), 179–181.

Cochran-Smith, M. (2001b). Learning to teach against the (new) grain. *Journal of Teacher Education, 52*(1), 279–310.

Cochran-Smith, M. (2001c). Reforming teacher education: Competing agendas. *Journal of Teacher Education, 52*(4), 263–265.

Cochran-Smith, M., & Lytle, S. (1999). Relationships of knowledge and practice: Teacher learning in communities. *Review of Research in Education, 24*(1), 249–305.

Cochran-Smith, M., & Lytle, S. (2009). *Inquiry as stance: Practitioner research for the next generation*. New

York, NY: Teachers College Press.

Colorado Education Initiative. (2020). *Student Perception Survey Toolkit*. The Colorado Education Initiative. Retrieved November 24, 2021, from https://www.coloradoedinitiative.org/Resources/student-perception-survey-toolkit/

Darling-Hammond, L. (2005). Teaching as a profession: Lessons in teacher preparation and professional development. *Phi Delta Kappan, 87*(3), 237–240.

Darling-Hammond, L., Burns, D., Campbell, C., Goodwin, A. L., Hammerness, K., Low, E. L., McIntyre, A.; Sato, M.; & Zeichner, K. (2017). *Empowered educators: How high-performing systems shape teaching quality around the world.* John Wiley & Sons.

Darling-Hammond, L., Hyler, M. E., & Gardner, M. (2017). *Effective teacher professional development*. Palo Alto: Learning Policy Institute.

Darling-Hammond, L., & McLaughlin, M. W. (1995). Policies that support professional development in an era of reform. *Phi Delta Kappan, 76*(8), 597-604.

Desimone, L. M., & Stuckey, D. (2014). Sustaining professional development. In L. Martin, S. Kragler, D. Quatroche, & K. Bauserman (Eds.), *Handbook of professional development in education: Successful models and practices, prek-12* (pp. 467-482). New York, NY: Guilford.

Díaz-Maggioli, G. (2004). *Teacher-centered professional development*. Virginia: Association for Supervision and Curriculum Development.

Didion, L., Toste, J. R., & Filderman, M. J. (2020). Teacher professional development and student reading achievement: A meta-analytic review of the effects. *Journal of Research on Educational Effectiveness, 13*(1), 29-66.

EVERY STUDENT SUCCEEDS ACT. Retrieved October 1, 2021, from https://www.congress.gov/114/plaws/publ95/PLAW-114publ95.pdf

Feldman, A. (1998). Implementing and assessing the power of conversation in the teaching of action research. *Teacher Education Quarterly*, 27-42.

Feldman, A. (1996). Enhancing the practice of physics teachers: Mechanisms for the generation and sharing of knowledge and understanding in collaborative action research. *Journal of Research in Science Teaching: The Official Journal of the National Association for Research in Science Teaching, 33*(5), 513-540.

Fletcher, S. (2012). Research mentoring teachers in intercultural education contexts; self-study. *International Journal of Mentoring and Coaching in Education, 1*(1), 66.

Fullan, M., Rincon-Gallardo, S., & Hargreaves, A. (2015). Professional capital as accountability. *Education Policy Analysis Archives, 23*(15), 1–17.

Foy, K., del Prado Hill, P., Patti, A., & Davis, J. (2018). Esperanza e imaginación: PDS partners working together to help bilingual middle school students build hope and imagination for their futures. *School-University Partnerships, 11*(1), 60-63.

Gabriel, R., Day, J. P., & Allington, R. (2011). Exemplary teacher voices on their own development. *Phi Delta Kappan, 92*(8), 37–41.

García, E., & Weiss, E. (2020). Examining the factors that play a role in the teacher shortage crisis: Key findings from EPI's' perfect storm in the teacher labor market series. *Economic Policy Institute.*

García, E., & Weiss, E. (2019). The role of early career supports, continuous professional development, and learning communities in the teacher shortage: The fifth report in the perfect storm in the teacher labor market series. *Economic Policy Institute.*

Garin, E., & Harper, M. (2016). A self-study investigation of using inquiry groups in a professional development school context. *School-University Partnerships, 9*(1), 54-63.

Gesel, S. A., LeJeune, L. M., Chow, J. C., Sinclair, A. C., & Lemons, C. J. (2021). A meta-analysis of the impact of professional development on teachers' knowledge, skill, and self-efficacy in data-based decision-making. *Journal of Learning Disabilities, 54*(4), 269-283.

Grundy, S. (1997). Participatory educational research in Australia: The first wave: 1976 to 1986. *Participatory Action Research: International Contexts and Consequences*, 125-150.

Harzing, A.W. (2007) *Publish or Perish*, available from https://harzing.com/resources/publish- or-perish

Hill, H. C. (2009). Fixing teacher professional development. *Phi Delta Kappan 90*(7), 470–477.

Ingersoll, R. M., and Collins, G. J. (2018). The status of teaching as a profession. In *Schools and Society: A Sociological Approach to Education*, 6th ed., edited by J. H. Ballantine, J. Z. Spade, and J. M. Stuber, 199–213. Los Angeles: SAGE.

Jensen, B, Sonnemann, J., Roberts-Hull, K. & Hunter, A. (2016). *Beyond PD: Teacher Professional Learning in High-Performing Systems*. National Center on Education and the Economy.

Johnston, S. (1994). Is action research a 'natural process for teachers? *Educational Action Research, 2*(1), 39-48.

24

Joubert, M., & Sutherland, R. (2008). *Researching CPD for teachers of mathematics: A review of the literature.* London: National Centre for Excellence in the Teaching of Mathematics.

Kemmis, S., McTaggart, R., & Nixon, R. (2014). A new view of research: Research within practice traditions. In *The action research planner* (pp. 67-83). Springer, Singapore.

Kraft, M. A., Blazar, D. & Hogan, D. (2018). The effect of teacher coaching on instruction and achievement: A meta-analysis of the causal evidence. *Review of Educational Research 88*(4), 547–558.

Lambirth, A., Cabral, A., McDonald, R., Philpott, C., Brett, A., & Magaji, A. (2021). Teacher-led professional development through a model of action research, collaboration and facilitation. *Professional Development in Education, 47*(5), 815-833.

Lewin, K. (1946) Action research and minority problems. *Journal of Social Issues 2*(4), 34–46.

Manzar-Abbas, S., & Lu, L. (2015). The Practicum Status in UE Campuses during B. Ed. Programme: TEs' Perceptions. *Journal of Research & Reflections in Education (JRRE), 9*(1).

Matsko, K. K., Ronfeldt, M., Nolan, H. G., Klugman, J., Reininger, M., & Brockman, S. L. (2020). Cooperating teacher as model and coach: What leads to student teachers' perceptions of preparedness?. *Journal of Teacher Education, 71*(1), 41-62.

Mertler, C.A. (2013) 'Classroom-based action research: revisiting the process as customizable and meaningful professional development for educators', *Journal of Pedagogic Development, 3*(3), 38-42.

Mertler, C. A. (2012) Action research: Improving schools and empowering educators (3rd ed.). Thousand Oaks, CA: Sage.

Milner, H. R., & Laughter, J. (2015). But good intentions are not enough: Preparing teachers to centre race and poverty. *Urban Review, 47*, 341–363.

Mizell, Hayes. 2010. *Why Professional Development Matters.* Learning Forward.

National Council for Accreditation of Teacher Education (2010), Transforming teacher education through clinical practice: a national strategy to prepare effective teachers, report of the Blue Ribbon Panel on Clinical Preparation and Partnerships for Improved Student Learning, NCATE, Washington, DC.

No Child Left Behind Act of 2001, P.L. 107–110, 20 U.S.C. § 6319 (2002)

PUBLIC LAW 114–95—DEC. 10, 2015. (2015, December 10). EVERY STUDENT SUCCEEDS ACT. Retrieved October 1, 2021, from https://www.congress.gov/114/plaws/publ95/PLAW-114publ95.pdf

Parker, A., Bush, A., & Yendol-Hoppey, D. (2016). Understanding teacher candidates' engagement with inquiry-based professional development: A continuum of responses and needs. *The New Educator, 12*(3), 221-242.

Petrie, K., & McGee, C. (2012). Teacher professional development: Who is the learner? *Australian Journal of Teacher Education, 37*, 59–72.

Reagan, E. M., Roegman, R., & Goodwin, A. L. (2017). Inquiry in the round? Education rounds in a teacher residency program. *Action in Teacher Education, 39*(3), 239-254.

Riel, M. M., & Rowell, L. L. (2017). Action research and the development of expertise: Rethinking teacher education. In *The Palgrave International Handbook of Action Research* (pp. 667-688). Palgrave Macmillan, New York.

Riel, M. (2019). Understanding Collaborative Action Research. Center For Collaborative Action Research, Pepperdine University CA, USA (Last revision Mar 2019). Accessed Online on (date) from http://cadres.pepperdine.edu/ccar/define.html.

Rogers, R. M. (2017). Deliberate investigations of a flipped class. *School-University Partnerships, 10*(4), 95-111.

Romijn, B. R., Slot, P. L., & Leseman, P. P. (2021). Increasing teachers' intercultural competences in teacher preparation programs and through professional development: A review. *Teaching and Teacher Education*, 98.

Sancar, R., Atal, D., & Deryakulu, D. (2021). A new framework for teachers' professional development. *Teaching and Teacher Education*, 101.

Saribas, D., & Akdemir, Z. G. (2020). Action research on preservice elementary teachers' understandings of the scientific method and the use of evidence in a science and technology teaching course. *Research in Science & Technological Education*, 1-23.

Schulte, A., & Klipfel, L. H. (2016, October). External influences on an internal process: Supporting preservice teacher research. In *The Educational Forum (80)*4, 457-465. Routledge.

Shanks, J. (2016). Implementing action research and professional learning communities in a professional development school setting to support teacher candidate learning. *School-University Partnerships, 9*(1), 45-53.

Sharkey, J., Olarte, A., & Ramirez, L. (2016). Developing a deeper understanding of community-based pedagogies with teachers: Learning with and from teachers in Colombia. *Journal of Teacher Education, 67*, 306–319.

Sims, S., & Fletcher-Wood, H. (2021). Identifying the characteristics of effective teacher professional development: a critical review. *School effectiveness and school improvement, 32*(1), 47-63.

Smith, J., & Nadelson, L. (2016). Learning for you and learning for me: Mentoring as professional development for mentor teachers. *Mentoring & Tutoring: Partnership in Learning, 24*(1), 59-72.

Somekh, B. (1993) Quality in educational research: the contribution of classroom teachers, in: J. Edge & K. Richards (Eds) *Teachers develop teachers research: papers on classroom research and teacher development* (Oxford, Heinemann).

US PREP. (2020). *Our Model*. US PREP Renewing Educator Preparation. Retrieved October 28, 2021, from https://www.usprepnationalcenter.com/portfolio-items/our-model/

Wei, R. C., Darling-Hammond, L., & Adamson, F. (2010). Professional development in the United States: Trends and challenges. *National Staff Development Council*, 1-4.

Wenger, E. (1998). *Communities of practice: Learning, meaning, and identity*. New York: Cambridge University Press.

West, C. (2011). Action research as a professional development activity. *Arts Education Policy Review, 112,* 89–94.

Wolkenhauer, R., & Hooser, A. (2021). Becoming clinically grounded teacher educators: Inquiry communities in clinical teacher preparation. *Journal of Teacher Education, 72*(2), 168-179.

Yigit, C., & Bagceci, B. (2017). Teachers' opinions regarding the usage of action research in professional development. *Journal of Education and Training Studies, 5*(2), 243-252.

Chapter 3

Introducing Preservice Teachers to Culturally Responsive Instruction

Charity Gamboa Embley, Ph.D.

Abstract

Professional development in the area of multicultural education tends to prepare institutional staff to work with diverse learners and implement a gender-fair or racial-fair educational program. However, when it comes to professional learning, there are important considerations that seem to be missing from multicultural education. When preservice teachers themselves have greater clarity on the intricacies of multicultural education, they are better equipped with knowledge to help students discover their own academic strengths, greater understanding of others' distinct characteristics, and a heightened level of interpersonal skills. To address these areas, Charity Embley will investigate the need to traverse challenges stemming from opposition to equality and diversity conversations. Additionally, she will describe the balance of providing critical cultural information for preservice teachers stemming from other ethnicities and protecting against stereotypes. Lastly, she will provide professional learning approaches to connect underlying multicultural education theories as part of an individual's agency to practice engagement with other learners.

Introduction

As an educator of a teacher education program in my college, I feel this immense responsibility to prepare my students to be culturally responsive teachers. I have attended numerous professional development training on culturally responsive teaching (CRT), and yet, the concept is re-purposed by institutions who advocate for college-readiness programs. But for a framework that advocates for inclusive learning, teachers are being convinced that once they acknowledge they have students of color, they have accomplished diversity training. In other words, the only category of diversity being connected to such training is synonymous with race. Thus, it is vital that we move CRT training among preservice teachers beyond race and connect them to more diverse issues in education. Moll et al. (1992) posit that we should gather the funds of knowledge that our students already have and utilize these potentials for classroom instruction. These funds of knowledge can actually be mapped into various subject matters.

Moreover, Gay's (2013) discussion on cultural responsiveness explained that culturally responsive teaching indicated what learning was relevant for students from various ethnic groups. For instance, what learning is for Asian Americans such as Filipinos, Chinese, Koreans, etc., differs conceptually from teaching Latinos, African-Americans and European-Americans. Thus, to define culturally responsive teaching is to use the "cultural knowledge, prior experiences, frames of reference, and performance of styles of ethnically diverse students to make learning encounters more relevant to and affective for them" (Gay, 2013, pp. 49–50). Gay (2013) also posits that the education of diverse students promoted in-school and out-of-school living, equality, and the development of student empowerment. In other words, it is important to accept that a community with diverse individuals exists and are coming from various cultural backgrounds.

The framework of culturally responsive teaching is meant to expand the knowledge of preservice teachers by modeling literacy practices that inculcate students' cultural experiences. These cultural experiences, especially their home experiences, are vital in connecting to their academic learning. This chapter is therefore meant to inform preservice teachers of the need to understand the tenets of multiculturalism as related to culturally responsive teaching, the need to include "youth culture" to the understanding of culture, and how funds of knowledge can be utilized to map each subject matter.

Multiculturalism and Beyond

Perception of multiculturalism must be understood beyond the mantra of people of color and must address what is unique to many groups, such as their language, family history, and overall experiences. The school experiences must also help students relate to various aspects of diversity. The intention, therefore, is to encourage people to work together and celebrate their differences (Association of Supervision and Curriculum Development, 2017). However, the perception of multiculturalism is marginalized if the approach is simply to use the concept as an addendum to core subject matters. The concept must be interdisciplinary and integrated into the current curriculum. The probable way that we could sincerely teach multiculturalism is if it is not superficial and its implementation is taught by trained teachers (Gay 2000/2004; Ladon-Billings, 1994).

Banks' (2001) dimensions of multicultural education clearly elucidates how multicultural education must be integrated into the curriculum. Examples from home experiences and various cultural groups can be used to explain concepts in subject areas. For instance, *sungka*, a traditional Filipino game, starts with 49 game pieces. These pieces may be marbles or shells and are equally distributed to alternate holes with seven pieces in every other hole, except the "heads," which must remain empty. Each player controls their own seven holes on their side and has control of the "head" to their right. The outcome of the game is to amass as many pieces as possible in each player's head. Playing *sungka* has been hailed as a great practice to foremost learn math and problem-solving skills. This game is also a great example of a cultural group that can harness memory and strategy skills.

Another aspect of Banks' (2001) dimension of multicultural education is seen in the way teachers guide students in actively questioning where knowledge comes from and even challenge the "universalist" claims of literature. Hogan (2016) explains that works in the domain of being "universalist" (or universals) recurred with greater tendency and even attempted to impose one's image over on everyone else. In keeping with this, it was essential to understand that the "universalist" claims were often subjected to the imposition of a local preference to the rest of the world. The point, according to Hogan (2016), was that it made no sense to claim that one language or particular was more universal than the other, nor claim that only one traditional should be implemented. This was the case for cultural representation. The examination of "uneven" or "disadvantaged" cultural representation is even at the center of postcolonial theory because of the relevance of this perspective within the modern arena of intellectual debate and innovation (Gandhi, 1998; Hawley, 2001; Hiddleston, 2009; Madsen,

2003).

Thus, in guiding students to actively question literature, students must be taught to not merely buy into the cultural assumptions held by most literature but to understand the biases of writers. Often, these biases influence the way knowledge is constructed (Banks, 2001). For instance, discourses pertaining to colonialism should question and scrutinize the contours of shifting power. Several cultural groups living in the U.S. were previously colonized by countries such as Great Britain, Spain, and the United States in their native country. There are immigrants in the United States (and all over the world presumably) who came from countries whose identities were shaped by their past ancestral history. It is irrational to homogenize immigrant identity into one model because immigrants have different identities based on their colonial past (Knake, 2014; Martin, 2002). If students are learning to question what they are reading, they also understand the complexity of otherness. In fact, some books do present the diversity of people's traditions and culture. If concepts of otherness or double consciousness are implied in such literature, students are able to discern the artificiality of sympathy and references to otherness and instead embrace their own rich culture and uniqueness.

One other aspect from Banks is the dimension of prejudice. According to Banks (2001), prejudice can be reduced if students develop positive and open racial attitudes. This means that the more students are involved in interracial contacts; they foster cooperation rather than competition and foster equality rather than subjugation. If school administrators, teachers, and parents are not sanctioning these interracial contacts, they, too, are reducing the prejudice in the school community. Most of the time, the actions of a certain social group that is regarded as the dominant group in the community can influence the way other people in the community will act. In the classroom, teachers are encouraged to foster interracial interaction in many ways, such as grouping students without any thoughts of race, introducing particular traditions and relating that to a subject matter concept; or introducing different traditions as weekly themes in, i.e., in the Homeroom class.

Moreover, Banks (2001) believed that an "equity pedagogy" dimension exists when teachers change the way they teach and facilitate the academic achievement of students from diverse racial groups. If teachers use different tools and materials that are within the learning range of various cultural groups, teachers can customize their teaching style to fit the needs of their diverse students. In Ladson-Billings (1994) articled entitled "What We Can Learn from Multicultural Education Research," she shared a story of two teachers by the names of Don Wilson and Margie Stewart. Wilson's class of 28 fourth graders were mostly composed of African-Americans and Latinos, and so, he did not attempt to push them too hard because their achievement levels were below national averages; while Stewart's class of 28 were mostly made up of 23 White and upper-middle-class children who tested above grade level (Ladson-Billings, 1994). Ladson-Billings (1994) points out that the students of color in Stewart's class lagged behind, with one particular student named Jose, who had limited English and was considered to be a special needs student because Stewart had to work with Jose on a one-on-one basis several times. How both Wilson and Stewart thought about their students had a profound effect on their student's performance in class. Teachers may have their own biases against students of color, particularly in expecting more from white upper-class students than from lower-class African-Americans or Latino students. Therefore, Ladson-Billings (1994) posits that teachers like Wilson and Stewart were not attributing their problems against students of color to ineffective teaching strategies.

The dimension in empowering school culture embodies the restructuring that was premised on mutual respect for cultural differences. Banks (2001) asserted that variables such as labeling practices, achievement gaps, rates of enrollment in special education among cultural groups, and the interaction of school personnel and students are important variables that need reformation. An empowered school is one that enables the practice of multicultural education by providing teachers ample opportunities to plan instruction together. Not only that, teachers become accountable for teaching all students, not just the privileged few. As Ladson-Billings (1994) reiterates, in order for teachers to be effective, they need to be prepared to teach children who are not White.

In a manner of speaking, the emphasis of culturally responsive teaching also encompasses teaching to the cultural diversity that can help students acquire more knowledge about the lives and challenges of other ethnic/racial groups. Awareness of cultural diversity, according to Gay (2013), is often denigrated in traditional schooling. Gay

(2013) underscored that the "positive learning possibilities of marginalized students and their heritage groups instead of belaboring their problems and pathologies" (pp. 50–51) is a great support system for a diverse population of students. In Ladson-Billings' (1994) account of Wilson and Stewart's teaching mentality, she exemplified how the outright racism caused these two teachers to hold negative beliefs about students of color instead of elevating their learning potentials.

Overall, even in the contemporary classroom, students who were not White-faced challenges, as at best teachers, were unprepared for the challenges of an ethnically diverse class during the 21st century. Gay (2004) underscores how teachers move hurriedly into integrating various lessons in the classroom without probing deeper into the particularities of a student's history. This sentiment indeed made me wonder how many of the lessons presented in mainstream K-12 classrooms actually considered the value these lessons play in the lives of ethnically diverse students.

Mastering Classroom Inclusion for Preservice Teachers

Ladson-Billings (1994) has reiterated and argued that teachers should not be merely satisfied with superficial approaches to teaching content. Banks (2001) also echoed this sentiment by emphasizing the need for schools to integrate materials that denote the infusion of cultural content inside the classroom. In other words, if we consider the arguments put forth by Banks and Ladson-Billings regarding the importance of instructional materials and pedagogy that are culturally receptive to ethnically diverse students, teachers are given access to at least one other culture inside their classrooms. In fact, students are leaving schools bi-culturally competent. However, it's important to note that multiculturalism is not just covering any student who is considered Black or Brown. White students should not go out into the global workforce and only understand themselves or their own culture (Ladson-Billings, 2017). Therefore, culturally relevant teaching is not simply about upholding the culture students come with but providing them the opportunity to understand other cultures, as well. This means that teachers are not simply trivializing the fact that diversity issues only come into play when there are festivals (Ladson-Billings, 1994).

In a *Public School Review* article written by Chen (2019), White students are now the minority in public schools. Of this population,

51% are racialized in public schools (Chen, 2019). In fact, Krogstad and Fry (2014) had already projected in 2014 that public schools in America are going to be majority-minority. Geiger (2017) explains that Hispanics, Asian Americans, and Pacific Islanders make up the growing share of the U.S. public school population. However, Klein (2017) posits that even if the majority of students entering public schools are minorities, most teachers are still White. This means that teacher demographics are simply shifting slower than student demographics. Since 2011, 82% of teachers (approximately 3.3 million) identified themselves as White in data reported by the Department of Education (2016). If such data reveals un-matching shifts between teachers and students in terms of demographics, how do we boost minority student engagement and achievement?

For preservice teachers entering the education field, student engagement and achievement are buzzwords. Every content learned inside the teacher education classrooms reveals different techniques in student engagement and success that can be employed in K-12 classrooms. However, preservice teachers have to be cognizant that they will be teaching a diverse population. Minero (2020) asserts that teachers, whether seasoned or preservice, do need to uncover their own implicit bias. Brownstein (2019) explains that implicit bias is when people act on their own prejudices without any intention. Minero (2020) shares that one educator felt it "was a struggle because growing up, it was instilled in me that Black Americans do not value hard work and only value the quick buck" (para. 9). Note that this kind of bias may also be shared by other teachers. Thus, Minero (2020) urges teachers to meet students where they are and where they have been.

One way they can have a better understanding of their students' experiences is by reading books (Preston, 2017), i.e., written by minority authors, perhaps developing a book club, and attending professional development training (which in my experience, offered book reading and discussion as part of our professional learning communities). Some good reads I highly suggest are *Beyond Heroes and Holidays* by Enid Lee, Deborah Menkart, and Margo Ozakawa-Rey (1998) that guides teachers on how to dismantle racism in schools; *Why Are All The Black Kids Sitting Together* in the Cafeteria by Beverly Daniel Tatum (2003) that speaks of the new way of thinking and talking about race; *The Dreamkeepers: Successful Teachers of African*

American Children by Gloria Ladson-Billings (1997) that highlights the experiences of eight African-American teachers; *The Spirit Catches You and You Fall Down—A Hmong Child, Her American Doctors,* and *The Collision of Two Cultures* by Anne Fadiman (1997) that outlines the history, struggles, and the emigration of the Hmong into the United States; and *Other People's Children: Cultural Conflict in the Classroom* by Lisa Delpit (1996) that suggests many of the problems encountered by students of color were a product of miscommunication between teachers and other people's children.

Another lens to look into boosting minority engagement and achievement is by avoiding code-switching and pervasive deficit thinking. Code-switching pertains to the mentality that minority students should be taught how to play the "game" of adopting White cultural norms. This is reminiscent of the notion of "otherness" that also includes "doubleness" or "double consciousness" (Cohen, 2008; Du Bois, 1903/2007). W.E.B. Du Bois (1903/2007) pointed to this double-consciousness as always looking at oneself through the eyes of others:

> One ever feels his two-ness, an American, a Negro; two souls, two thoughts, two un-reconciled strivings; two warring ideals in one dark body, whose dogged strength alone keeps it from being torn asunder. (p. 2)

This "doubleness" was also evident from Fanon's (1967) claims in *Black Skin White Mask* that although the Black man wanted to be recognized for his own worth, "the Black man [wanted] to be White" (p. 9). DiAngelo (2018) also refers to this term as "passing"— an ability to blend in as a White person (p. xvi). The Black man insisted that he wanted to prove to the White man his equal value of intellect (Fanon, 1967). Imagine the damage done to young children if they are indoctrinated into the notion of double consciousness to adopt the majority culture—school children would have an extremely difficult task of extricating themselves from this consciousness.

Corollary, pervasive deficit thinking holds marginalized individuals from historically oppressed populations that they are responsible for any inequalities and injustices they have experienced in their lives. Students in this pervasive deficit mindset are supposedly held responsible for such failures because of their family and community background. For instance, teachers often have this tendency to think that students who are labeled as "at-risk" are most likely to fail because their lack of character or strength is responsible for any educational challenges they face in their lives. Although society sometimes may construct "at-risk" students as economically poor, their family background may be full of cultural and linguistic wealth. Some educators assume that students who are "at-risk" may not have the adversity to overcome their challenges. In fact, cultural and linguistic wealth evident in families is what could fuel "at-risk" students into overcoming challenges.

All in all, it is always important to track students for graduation, whether they are minorities or not. Chen (2019) postulates that nationally, only 78% of students graduate from high school on time. It is far worse for minorities, with 66% of African-American students and 69% of Indigenous American students who graduate with their class (Chen, 2019). Whether students (minority or not) are facing adversities in life, it is up to the teacher to profoundly know their students better. In fact, it takes a lot of determination and commitment to be able to find the time to get to know students. Teachers nowadays are exhausted because of the pressure of teaching the test and are evidently rated based on test scores. Such high-stakes accountability has depleted teachers' energy, and they are spending less time and attention on their students. However, it is never an excuse to say "I have no time" when it comes to the future of our school children. Preservice teachers need to be aware that they are now facing a very diverse classroom—one that needs their attention and time, aside from the immense reality of high-stakes accountability.

Need to Understand the Prevalence of Youth Culture

Teachers and students grew up in different generations. This reality is important in understanding how each generation tackles day-to-day issues. This is where the notion of youth culture comes in. Youth culture refers to the ways that adolescents conduct their day-to-day activities. These ways are evident in their interests, manner/style of dressing, behaviors in and out of school, choice of music, language or lingo, and dating beliefs. Note that the concept of youth culture pertains to all generations, and conversations about youth culture should be tackled within contemporary society. But also note that whatever generation gap there is between teachers and students must also be discussed within the premise that generations may have different or similar experiences that could also influence their own system of beliefs. For instance, individuals who grew up in the 60s and 70s experienced the hippie culture—a countercultural movement that started in U.S. college/university campuses.

This countercultural movement basically spurned mainstream American life. Other youth culture examples include hairstyles exhibiting nonconformity to mainstream society; trending music genres wherein teenagers are able to validate their emotions; behavior such as smoking and drinking that is not expected by parents; language that is considered as "cool;" and unacceptable academic performance to conform to peer pressure. In addition, the notion of youth culture is easily understood because each different generation will have their own youth culture that is reflective of their own time. Thus, it is natural to assume that in discovering one's own identity, one is able to seek out others of the same age group to learn and understand society's expectations. Hence, we often refer to Erik Erikson's question of, "Who am I?"

The prevalence of youth culture is evident in activities that bring teenagers together. Teenagers like to gather as a group. This social gathering was really emphasized when the school became compulsory and societal changes such as hanging out in a coffee shop when coffee drinking (e.g., frappes, non-alcoholic shaken drinks, etc.) became such a current trend among teenagers. It used to be that teenagers would prefer to gather socially in a mall (which they still do) or in a snack bar.

So, what can preservice teachers learn from youth culture? Nowadays, youth culture is synonymous with the understanding of technological determinism (Mesch, 2019). The Internet is considered an innovative force that influences the youth because of how teenagers are able to express themselves and communicate with others. These are teenagers (digital natives) who were born in a media-rich environment—holding electronic devices all the time, using digital spaces for interacting with others, and expressing their identities in social media. They are talented in technology and their immersion in technology influences their ideas and interests that will have a profound impact on their future lives. In other words, teenagers can process their beliefs differently from their predecessors, who may have different beliefs in technology as them. This is indeed a challenge that preservice teachers may face as they journey into the classrooms.

Hip Hop's Longevity in Understanding the Youth

Another note that Ladson-Billings (2021) emphasizes in our changing and diverse contemporary society is to recognize the longevity and power of hip-hop culture. Hip hop culture was developed in the early 70s by African Americans, Latinos, and Caribbean Americans in the Bronx, New York (The Kennedy Center, 2020). It describes an art movement that is composed of chest-thumping beats and dance steps. Hip hop is also composed of *jing* as an artistic exploration of beats and music; of rapping by synthesizing poetry to a beat; of breaking as a dance form; of graffiti as a form of painting; of combining the elements of drama, stories, and poetry into the hip hop elements to portray a form of literature and theater; and of integrating moral and spiritual principles (hip hop "being") as a way to know more about the self (The Kennedy Center, 2020).

The longevity of hip hop is also premised on its philosophy of identity and the ways to express that identity (The Kennedy Center, 2020). Knowing where one comes from will show one where you are going. This way, when one knows where you are going, it will lead one to understand what to learn. The hip-hop philosophy also places great importance on one's own education.

However, hip hop is considered to have a fickle fan base (The Kennedy Center, 2020). Nowadays, songs have a faster reach to the public through streaming platforms. New songs are presented daily, and people have multiple opportunities to like, follow and purchase songs. So, out with the old and in with the new. Does hip hop have the ability to influence the next generation? This question can only be answered based on how fans are able to keep its momentum going. If one still listens to its music and embraces its culture, then it is alive. But with a pickle fan base, hip hop's longevity may not be as everlasting.

How many of our preservice teachers are aware of hip hop's influence on our culture? How can they embed its philosophy in their understanding of student engagement and achievement? The culture of hip hop does place importance on education. If this concept is understood by most preservice teachers who may also have an idea of the hip-hop music they listened to, why not integrate the hip-hop culture as an innovative way of presenting instructional activities? This is indeed something to consider when planning lessons.

Remembering Madison Avenue

How many of our young preservice teachers even know about Madison Avenue? It is located in the boroughs of Manhattan, New York City. But how many of them have even been to New York City? This question might be moot to this discussion, but it is a thought to ponder when activating prior experiences among our preservice teachers. However, having been to Madison Avenue is not relevant. The most vital part is knowing that Madison Avenue started an artistic revolution when it comes to advertising, but issues of race have come to the attention of a few. In 1968, the New York Commission on Human Rights held discrimination hearings in television and radio advertising (The National Museum of American History Behring Center, n.d.). It was discovered that only 3.5% of African Americans were employed in advertising agencies even if the Special Markets Divisions of ad agencies were composed of African Americans and Latinos who studied racial minorities and how to sell to them (The National Museum of American History Behring Center, n.d.). In the end, advertising executives believed that they needed to change the feel of advertising by using minority representations as representatives of ethnic consumers.

Building Cultural Competence

The foremost question we ask ourselves in the teacher education program is—how do we help teachers understand disparity? Previously, we discussed adversities minorities face every day, youth culture, and even the effects of racial issues in Madison Avenue. However, in this era of COVID-19, how do we emphasize cultural competence among preservice teachers and prepare them for the societal changes brought about by the pandemic?

According to the National Association for Multicultural Education (2021), there are instructional essentials that could help educators enact culturally responsive teaching and opportunities to examine educational resources to support educators in the classroom. For preservice teachers there is a need to be aware of the growing population of minorities in the U.S. and must consider what culturally responsive teaching looks like in their future classrooms. This entails learning more about their students' background and where students are actually "coming from." Foremost, there is a need to treat students as competent. Although some students might speak with an accent or have "halting" English because English is not their first language, it does not mean they are academically incompetent. Being a bilingual myself, I had no issues understanding academic content. My uncertainty stems from speaking English because I get embarrassed if I mispronounce English words. I would tell my preservice teachers that my brain has an "off" and "on" switch because I have to reset my brain whenever I am switching languages. I switch languages because it depends on who I converse with. But there was nothing wrong with my comprehension—it is just uncanny that some people would equate non-English speakers as those who are inept. I assume that my own experiences would also mimic other minorities who are bilingual. The best course that preservice teachers must know is not to make sweeping generalizations. Treat every student as competent regardless of their race and language.

As I mentioned earlier, each student brings different experiences into the classroom. Those experiences are meaningful because they offer glimpses of how our students learn. Hence, build on students' real-life experiences and use those experiences when planning lessons. Teachers tend to pick instructional activities from textbooks or online materials and think they are sufficient for teaching. But that is not enough—there is a need to scrutinize if such resources are applicable to your classroom population.

If you give an example of a problem-solving question, ensure that your students are familiar with specific scenarios. Here is an example: "A family was driving to their cabin, and their car broke down at the bottom of the mountain. There was also an ensuing blizzard. Afraid of being stuck in the cold, the family decided to seek help. They saw the light coming from a cabin somewhere on the mountain. How can they reach the cabin without any hiking equipment?" After analyzing this example, how can teachers make this example relevant to their students? Have your students ever experienced a blizzard? If so, ask them to describe a blizzard. If not, how will you scaffold this particular scenario so your students can connect to the problem at hand? Or customize the scenario to meet your students' prior knowledge. If your community has never experienced a blizzard, how about a sandstorm or a hurricane? Thus, choose examples that your students can empathize with so they can relate them to their real-life experiences.

The same instance of using relevant example questions may also be similar when choosing literature for reading exercises in your classroom. In my class, I expose my students to books written by minority authors or books that are bilingual. My modular topic on lesson planning entails choosing and devising a plan to teach a book. This is the sole reason why my office and the home library are full of young adult literature, children's books and varying novels are written mostly by minority authors. In my research, I discovered that libraries in my county have little or none of the bilingual or literature is written by minority authors (Embley, 2020). I collected books and allowed my preservice teachers to choose from this set as part of their lesson planning activity. They also have to demo teach their lesson plan. My intention is to solely allow my preservice teachers to become aware that literature should be chosen carefully to broaden the conception of literacy for students regardless of race. If minority students are able to read books and relate to the characters, they would have more interest in their own unique culture. At the same time, other students are also benefiting from understanding another culture.

Two years ago, I discovered a book entitled *Journey for Justice—Life of Larry Itliong*, written by Filipino-American historian Dawn Mabalon and illustrated by Gayle Romasanta (2018). This book highlights the story of farmworker Larry Itliong who worked alongside Cesar Chavez during the 1956 farm labor union strike in Stockton, California. Contrary to popular belief, it was Itliong's idea to start the strike, and he partnered with Cesar Chavez to gain momentum because of Chavez's popularity. Historical books have not highlighted Itliong and other Filipino farm workers' contributions to this event. Filipino and Mexican farmworkers struggled and fought alongside each other in this large-scale agricultural strike. This is information that students, regardless of race, must know. It is also a moment for Filipino students to acknowledge their own grit. Note that when the agricultural strike happened in 1956, Larry Itliong was much older and Cesar Chavez was a young and vibrant Mexican hero. Itliong realized that he needed to take a back seat because of his age. Imagine if a Filipino student takes a back seat similarly to Itliong because he or she seems like the most tenuous leader in the classroom. How can teachers cultivate the future of students who seem tenuous as leaders? Well, give opportunities for students of color to become leaders in the classroom. This is not about being allowed to pass papers or being the favorite student to do errands for the teacher. It is about being taught to become a leader in small group discussions. Students can take turns to become leader, writer, or discussant. By rotating roles among students, the teacher is giving everyone an opportunity to be a strong leader.

Furthermore, there is substance when teachers and students engage in collective struggle. The pandemic has opened the eyes of students regarding political issues and the social and economic struggles of families. Students' parents may have lost their jobs, and this is applicable to all students. It is vital that students learn to respect others and discern what is right and wrong from videos they see on social media outlets. All over the country, there are countless people who have opinions, people who enact violence against other races (e.g., Asian Americans), and people who simply attack others because of race and language. K-12 students have access to these realities because of their access to social media. It is important to have these conversations between teachers and students so both can be culturally competent and find common ground to agree and disagree.

Mapping Funds of Knowledge

Moll et al. (1992) were spot-on when they postulated that an analysis of the funds of knowledge that students already have in their lives represents a realistic view of their own households as cultural resources that have the potential for classroom instruction. In fact, Moll et al. further claim that "This view of households, we should mention, contrasts sharply with prevailing views of working-class families as disorganized socially and deficient intellectually" (p. 134). In essence, the funds of knowledge implied in this chapter are simply the household knowledge that students already have and can bring to the classroom as their real experiences. Examples of these funds of knowledge may be the ways a family describes, imbibes, and reacts to certain tasks: expression of religion, family stories, immigration routes, medical procedures (use of herbal medicine), child-rearing practices, attitude towards pets, music choices (folk music), industry skills (carpentry, woodworking), and etc.

Such is the case that when preservice teachers (regardless of content to be taught) understand where students' knowledge comes from, they are able to map these household funds of knowledge against their own subject area. When it comes to science, teachers can use students' knowledge of animal management, farming ideas, or fixing/repairing mechanical equipment as examples in biology, chemistry, and physics. For math, the way other families shop, budget, or manage their finances could be examples in accounting or statistics. For literacy, family tales, stories, and photos could be used in narratives for English writing activities or oral discussions in literature classes. For social studies, immigration routes for families who migrated to the U.S. can be compared to the historical migration of early settlers and can be used as examples in geography and history classes. For health classes, family knowledge or use of alternative medicine, herbal medicine, and childcare beliefs could be used as examples in physical education and consumer science classes. Not to be excluded is in the arts when folk music, carpentry, and woodworking designs could be examples in painting, sculpting, or music classes.

All of the examples noted above do take some planning and timing. The important gesture that preservice teachers must inculcate is that they try to integrate these examples in their classes as the need arises. But before any mapping can be done, challenge preservice teachers to do a walk around the neighborhood area of where they possibly want to teach. Spend time walking around while observing the structures (shapes of buildings), plant life, geological structures, types of stores, availability of playgrounds (and watch what games children play if you see any), and listen to any sounds or noises. Make a mental list or write your observations in a journal. These would be helpful in building a lesson based on the neighborhood. In a way, you are helping teach your students from their neighborhood and understand concepts in your own subject matter. Remember that whatever you see that is related to an academic concept are always ideas to build a curriculum.

Implications of Culturally Responsive Teaching for Pre-Service Teachers

Can we, therefore, ascertain that today's education will be the education of the future? As educators, we must critically assess our current instruction and determine various ways to address the different challenges we encounter in these changing times. If we are to prepare our future teachers, we can no longer depend on traditional teaching ideas. If we are to transform education to enhance the experiences of both our future teachers and students, we are allowing improvements in our educational system. We are also improving the delivery of quality education with innovative models.

Around the country, teachers have been made aware of culturally responsive teaching. Teachers are learning to connect home and academic cultures, as well as encourage students to imbibe social change. At the same, preservice and schoolteachers are given opportunities to reflect on themselves and develop opportunities for students to explore diversity. However, how extensive are these opportunities? Are these movements mere lip service to appease calls for diversity? Are schoolteachers and leaders simply satisfying such requirements for diversity and then assure themselves that they have fulfilled their duties? If we are on this pedestal, then we are not inculcating a culture of acceptance and recognition. It is a "must" that we prepare preservice teachers for such responsibilities and get them into the movement with real intentions. So how do we integrate these practices with genuine intention? Foremost, the integration of culturally relevant teaching has benefits that should be wholly understood.

When integrated into the classroom, culturally relevant teaching can strengthen students' sense of ethnic identity and pride. Muniz (2019) reported that a study of 315 middle and high school students who had opportunities to experience culturally responsive teaching developed a profound sense of racial identity—due to greater interest and engagement with learning that eventually led to better grades. Students were also able to safeguard themselves from stereotyping and discrimination (Muniz, 2019). It is possible that students may feel confused about their own identity and affect their school performance if they do not have opportunities to explore their own racial identity.

Culturally relevant teaching can also promote a sense of security for students inside the classroom. When teachers demonstrate they care about their students' individual needs and respect their own cultural identity, students feel a sense of belongingness. At the same time, it relates school concepts to everyday experiences. These connections make learning more meaningful to students. There is also an affirmation that their cultures and others matter.

Culturally relevant teaching also supports critical thinking among students. Teachers who connect real-life issues bring awareness to students regarding social justice. For instance, project-based learning has been a great approach in team-building and problem-solving when teachers use real-life scenarios and allow students to develop authentic solutions to such problems. Muniz (2019) gave an example of how seventh- and eighth-grade Latinx students used data from a traffic stop to understand racial profiling in their community while also learning math concepts. Through investigations, students are engaged in ways to analyze data, hypothesize and formulate solutions. Moreover, and most importantly, engage students in course materials that are relevant to their culture. In fact, books are great resources wherein students can identify with the relevant culture and characters of the books. Activities can be integrated into any lesson plans from students' home funds of knowledge.

Overall, when working with teacher education programs, we need to prepare preservice teachers to advocate for diversity, equity, and social justice. Programs should inadvertently commit to the diverse needs of students. Teachers must equip themselves with proper knowledge on inclusiveness and implement these practices into their classrooms. Teachers must reflect on their own practices, especially their own biases. If teachers are able to become aware and understand themselves and the identities of their students, they themselves can influence and transform the thinking of people around them and other teachers. All teachers need are spaces to question their assumptions, defy stereotypes and expose ignorance. Thus, if teachers are better prepared to face challenges in their careers, they can activate their voice and fight for those who are not able to fight.

References

Banks, J.A. (2001). Multicultural education: its effects on students' racial and gender role attitudes. In Banks, J.A. & Banks, C.A.M. (Eds), *Handbook of research on multicultural education*. San Francisco, CA: Jossey-Bass

Brownstein, M. (2019, July 13). *Implicit bias.* https://plato.stanford.edu/entries/implicit-bias/

Chen, G. (2019, October 14). *White students are now the minority in U.S. public schools.* https://www.public-schoolreview.com/blog/white-students-are-now-the-minority-in-u-s-public-schools

Cohen, R. (2008). Global diasporas: An introduction. New York, NY: Routledge.

DiAngelo, R. (2018). *White fragility why it's so hard for White people to talk about racism.* Boston, MA: Beacon Press.

Du Bois, W. E. B. (2007). The souls of black folk. New York, NY: Cosimo Classics.

Embley, C.G. (2020, April). K-12 literature with a Filipino flavor. *Teacher Librarian: The Journal for School*

Library Professionals, 47(4), 18–22.

Fanon, F. (1967). *Black skin, white masks.* New York City, NY: Grove Press

Foster, T. (n.d.). *What does longevity look like in today's hip-hop era?* https://www.wyexpect.com/stories/longevity-in-today-hip-hop

Gandhi, L. (1998). *Postcolonial theory a critical introduction.* New York, NY: Columbia University Press.

Gay, G. (2000). The importance of multicultural education. *Educational Leadership, 61*(4).

Gay, G. (2000). *Culturally responsive teaching.* New York: Teachers College Press.

Gay, G. (2013). Teaching to and through cultural diversity. *Curriculum Inquiry,43*(1), 48–70.

Geiger, A.W. (2017, October 25). Many minority students go to schools where at least half of their peers are their race or ethnicity. https://www.pewresearch.org/fact-tank/2017/10/25/many-minority-students-go-to-schools-where-at-least-half-of-their-peers-are-their-race-or-ethnicity/

Govinnage, S. (2015, April 24). *I read books by only minority authors for a year. It showed me how White our reading world is.* https://www.washingtonpost.com/posteverything/wp/2015/04/24/i-only-read-books-by-minority-authors-for-a-year-it-showed-me-just-how-white-our-reading-world-is/

Hawley, J. C. (Ed.). (2001). *Encyclopedia of postcolonial studies.* Westport, CT: Greenwood Press.

Hiddleston, J. (2009). *Understanding postcolonialism.* Stocksfield, UK: Acumen.

Klein, R. (2017, December 06). *A majority of students entering school this year are minorities, but most teachers are still white.* https://www.huffpost.com/entry/student-teacher-demographics_n_5738888?guccounter=1

Knake, J.M. (2014). Education means liberty: Filipino students, pensionados and U.S. colonial education. Western Illinois Historical Review, 6, 1–13.

Krogstad, J.M., & Fry, R. (2014, August 08). *Dept. of Ed projects public schools will be 'majority-minority' this fall.* https://www.pewresearch.org/fact-tank/2014/08/18/u-s-public-schools-expected-to-be-majority-minority-starting-this-fall/

Ladson-Billings, G. (1994). What we can learn from multicultural education research. *Educational Leadership,51*(8),22–26

Madsen, D. (2003). *Beyond the borders American literature and post-colonial theory.* Sterling, VA: Pluto Press

Martin, I.P. (2002). Pedagogy: Teaching practices of American colonial educators in the Philippines. *Kritika Kultura, 1*, 90–100.

Mesch, G. (2009). *The internet and youth culture.* Retrieved from https://hedgehogreview.com/issues/youth-culture/articles/the-internet-and-youth-culture

Moll, L. C., Amanti, C., Neff, D., & González, N. (1992). Funds of knowledge for teaching: Using a qualitative approach to connect homes and classrooms. *Theory into Practice, 31*(2), 132-141.

Minero, E. (2020, January 17). *Reflections on becoming more culturally responsive.* https://www.edutopia.org/article/reflections-becoming-more-culturally-responsive

Muniz, J. (2019, September 23). 5 ways culturally responsive teaching benefits learners. https://www.newamerica.org/education-policy/edcentral/5-ways-culturally-responsive-teaching-benefits-learners/

National Museum of American History Behring Center. (n.d.). Madison avenue, 1940's-1960's. https://americanhistory.si.edu/advertising-business/madison-avenue

Preston, T. (2017, June 29). *100 must-read classics by people of color.* https://bookriot.com/100-must-read-classics-by-people-of-color/

The Kennedy Center. (2020). *Hip-hop: A culture of vision and voice.* https://www.kennedy-center.org/education/resources-for-educators/classroom-resources/media-and-interactives/media/hip-hop/hip-hop-a-culture-of-vision-and-voice/

The National Association of Multicultural Education. (2021). *Principles of culturally relevant teaching.* https://www.nameorg.org/learn/principles_of_culturally_relev.php

U.S. Department of Education. (2016, July). *The state of racial diversity in the educator workforce* (Rep.). Washington, D.C: Policy and Program Studies Service Center Office of Planning, Evaluation and Policy Department. https://www2.ed.gov/rschstat/eval/highered/racial-diversity/state-racial-diversity-workforce.pdf

Chapter 4

Uniting Families and Classrooms through Inclusive Literacy Practices

Lindsay Malootian & Yvonne Cásares Khan

Abstract

Professional learning, especially for educators, requires ongoing reflection and adjustment of mindset to inform curriculum design and classroom instruction. This chapter illustrates the importance of shifting ways of thinking to make literacy connections with students' families, as families are stakeholders in education yet often excluded from decision-making in classrooms. The chapter first examines deficit thinking in teacher-centered relationships then introduces strategies to build open communication with students and families. Finally, the authors offer a variety of techniques and practices to establish literacy-based relationships between families and classrooms, with additional consideration of bilingual students' needs.

Introduction

Readers have the opportunity to become more proficient professional learners by putting into practice the inclusive strategies and activities outlined by the authors. Lindsay Malootian is an experienced middle school English teacher who has worked with many diverse groups of students and their families in Massachusetts. Yvonne Cásares Khan is a teacher recruiter and academic advisor in Texas. She grew up as a Spanish-speaking English language learner (ELL), and as a result of her lived experiences and a lifelong dream, she became a bilingual teacher. She passionately dedicated 32 years of her life working with Spanish-speaking ELLs in bilingual, self-contained classrooms. Both authors are working toward their Ph.D.'s in curriculum and instruction in the Language, Diversity, and Literacy Studies program at

Texas Tech University.

Deficit Thinking and Teacher-Centered Relationships

While it would be amiss to pin the manifestations of deficit thinking on any particular action or behavior, it is important in this chapter to explain the role of deficit thinking in teacher-centered relationships. In a teacher-centered classroom, instruction is conducted in a transmissionist format, an outdated approach by which knowledge is transmitted from the teacher to the students. In other words, the teacher is in charge of imparting their knowledge to learners driven by the underlying beliefs that knowledge acquisition is a "one-way street," and knowledge is drawn from only one perspective. This is particularly damaging to students—and students' families—whose sources of knowledge are different from those of the teacher's, especially if teachers do not take any responsibility for students' low achievement or failures on statewide achievement tests (García & Guerra, 2004).

Fortunately, the traditional teacher-centered classroom dynamic has gradually been losing traction, stemming from a groundbreaking study by Moll et al. (1992) that posited the integration of community resources in the classroom engages students of diverse backgrounds and experiences and promotes higher quality classroom instruction. While there is evidence that teaching models have been shying away from teacher-centered education, "The relationship between school staff and parents, however, has not seen such a move away from transmissionist models of behaviour" (Goodall, 2018, p.604). When a teacher's knowledge does not embrace or integrate the knowledge students acquire from their families or from other influential figures and settings outside of school, the teacher may subconsciously engage in deficit thinking.

One broad definition of deficit thinking as it applies to the teacher-centered classroom as outlined by García and Guerra (2004):"They [teachers] believe that the students and the families are at fault because, from their perspective, 'these children enter school without the necessary prerequisite knowledge and skills and those so-called uncaring parents neither value nor support their child's education" (García & Guerra, 2004, p. 151). Using this definition as a framework, teachers need to frequently reflect on the idea of prerequisite knowledge: *Whose knowledge is a priority in the classroom? What is prior knowledge to my students, and how does it differ from my own?* Additionally, the second part of this definition focuses on teachers' perceptions of parents' role in education. Deficit thinking holds students' families responsible for failures, yet teachers also need to reflect often about this issue: *What am I doing to engage my students' families in their child's education?* Engagement must entail interaction beyond a transmissionist style of education. In the classroom and beyond, engagement cannot be a one-sided discussion in which the teacher disseminates information to students' families and discourages mutual exchanges of ideas, concerns, or questions.

Without any effort to change the dynamics of the problematic yet common relationship between teachers and families—in which teachers perceive their knowledge as the most important, with minimal (if any) consideration or incorporation of various diverse demographic, linguistic, and socioeconomic viewpoints—educators perpetuate an underlying cycle of deficit thinking. Goodall (2018) asserted that teachers need to work closely with students' families; otherwise, "efforts to improve attainment are unlikely to be as fruitful as they could be, particularly for students from lower socioeconomic backgrounds, who are often at risk of underachievement in the current system" (pp. 604–605). In the next section, the authors describe literacy practices that can build relationships between students' families and educators.

Mindset Adjustment: Strategies for Building Relationships in Literacy Practices

At this point, a concerned educator might be asking themselves, "How can I combat deficit thinking in my relationships with students and their families? What can I do to bridge the gap between my own knowledge and my students' knowledge?" While the answer is seemingly simple, it has many complex parts: integrate students' knowledge, cultures, and experiences in pedagogical practices for literacy instruction and subject area content. This is known as culturally responsive teaching, which was introduced to the increasingly diverse education landscape by Ladson-Billings (1994). Culturally responsive teaching can be practiced in a variety of ways, and practices often look different from class to class (and even from student to student). The authors of this chapter offer research-informed suggestions based on their own teaching experiences, though Yvonne's practices are especially noteworthy, considering her background as both a bilingual student and a former teacher of many bilingual classrooms.

The first step to inhibit deficit thinking is to actively build positive working relationships with families to learn about the significant people, places, and activities in their lives. Learning this information opens new doors for teachers to connect with students and their families beyond a superficial level; as Moll et al. (1992) explained, "The typical teacher-student relationship seems 'thin' and 'single-stranded,' as the teacher 'knows' the students only from their performance within rather limited classroom contexts" (p. 134). Furthermore, traditional roles for family member involvement in schools are limiting as well, given that positions, such as event chaperones or volunteers, "[serve] only the school's agenda by doing the things educators expect them to do" (Pushor, 2010, p. 9). One way to establish genuine relationships is to schedule a home visit with students' families, if possible. Teachers or school administrators might prefer to meet at a location that is more convenient or comfortable for families, such as a local park, library, or ice cream shop. Heinrichs (2015) asserted that home visits could be beneficial to the budding partnership between families and teachers, offering the following guidelines to keep in mind:

> An initial phone call to each of the families is important... It is essential that teachers explain that the visit is focused on meeting the child and learning from the parent about their child in order for the teacher to teach the child to the best of her/his ability. The message that the teacher wants to portray is that the parent has the most knowledge of this child and is the expert; the teacher is coming to learn from this expertise. (p. 223)

For students' parents, home visits provide rich opportunities not only to share knowledge about their child but also to learn more about their child's teachers. Yvonne recounts that her experiences with home visits had ultimately been positive in relationship building, and parents often expressed their gratitude for her desire to create a constructive environment for their children. Home visits also helped Yvonne better understand the roles of students in their families by seeing them beyond the conventional, one-dimensional scope of the classroom. For more information on the processes, benefits, and experiences of home visits, suggested readings include Miller Marsh and Turner-Vornbeck (2010) and Ferlazzo and Hammond (2009). If, for some reason, teachers are unable to participate in-home visits, they are encouraged to engage in dialogues with families through phone calls or online video meetings. These methods of communication invite back-and-forth conversation in real-time: in other words, they discourage the single-sidedness of the transmissionist format, which is more typical in practices such as emailing or sending home class newsletters.

Educators should remember that these visits—whether virtual or in-person—serve multiple purposes, which leads to the second step in combating deficit thinking: use the newly acquired information about students and their families to develop a literacy curriculum infused with topics that are meaningful to the students. For example, if a teacher discovers that many students enjoy baseball, they should incorporate stories, figures, or news articles about baseball into their lesson plans or class routines. If a teacher does not understand the mechanics of baseball or knows the major players of today, they should ask their students; students will want to share knowledge about topics that are important to their lives! Take a couple of minutes each day to learn from students. They will usually be excited to share something they care about with their teachers, which can strengthen relationships in the classroom and beyond.

Simple Strategies for Promoting Literacy Development

As soon as teachers take steps to minimize deficit thinking, they shift from a teacher-centered classroom to a student-centered classroom and can utilize a number of strategies to promote literacy development. One strategy is to offer choices whenever possible. For example, if an English teacher has students who love different kinds of animals or own pets, they should provide multiple leveled texts about animals to meet the English standards or learning targets. There is always more than one text, question, model, or anecdote a teacher can use to address their objectives. While it may be tempting to revert to the "standard" lesson plans and materials because of a teacher's familiarity with them, remember that branching out helps to combat deficit thinking because teachers must make deliberate choices that are relevant to their current group of students. Students will improve their literacy skills if they are learning about something they find interesting or important. This is not a new concept, though it manifests itself in many ways. Dewey (2001) posited that students learn from a curriculum into which their personal experiences are integrated, stating that the teacher must,

> [...] abandon the notion of subject-matter as something fixed and ready-made in itself, outside the child's experience; cease thinking of the child's experience as also something hard and fast; see it as something fluent, embryonic, vital, and we realize that the child and the curriculum are simply two limits which define a single process. (p. 109)

In other words, student and family relationships are the foundations of developing literacy in the classroom: from these relationships, teachers can learn what is meaningful to students, and teachers can use what they learn about students outside of the classroom to engage them in class.

Literacy Bags

Another tool that teachers can use to bridge the gap between families and school literacy practices is to assemble and send home literacy bags. Literacy bags, also known as book bags, are the foundation of a school-to-home program that promotes family bonding over literacy activities such as reading, playing games (e.g., sight word bingo, rhyme I-Spy, alliteration memory), and writing in playful and collaborative ways (see Brand et al., 2014 and Leavitt-Noble & Grande, 2012). These bags are most suitable for K-5 (elementary) students and consist of three parts: reading material, two to three activities to accompany the reading, and explicit instructions for participating in the activities (make sure that reading materials and instructions are available in the languages that students use at home).

Prior to implementing literacy bags, be sure that families understand their purpose: families are more likely to participate if they fully conceptualize the benefits of the program. When parents or guardians understand their roles, they will eventually realize the advantages of regular literacy interactions with their child, which include enhanced language development, progress in building good reading habits, and opportunities for children and families to learn more about each other (Richardson et al., 2008). Brand et al. (2014) claimed,

> [...] families who have access to home–school literacy bags have increased engagement in home literacy activities with their children, garnered new ideas for meaning-

fully engaging their children in literacy activities, and acquired a better understanding of the importance of reading together with children. (p. 168)

Keep in mind these bags are intended to strengthen connections among family members, using literacy learning as a platform—it is necessary to have students' funds of knowledge integrated into readings and activities. Select texts based on what is learned about students and their families or encourage families to use books they enjoy: remember, teachers do not want to impose their own ideas of "good books," as this would resemble a transmissionist format of teaching. Activities should align with topics, themes, skills, and/or standards taught at school. It is also important to know that literacy bags can be used in any content area; literacy extends beyond language arts! For example, math literacy bags can tackle skills such as counting money and telling time by using culturally relevant word problems and activities for engagement.

Lessons of Literacy Beyond Classroom Walls

Gloria Ladson-Billings (1995), the pioneer of culturally relevant pedagogy (especially pertaining to the education of African American students), would often share her research findings with educators to help them integrate best teaching practices for diverse student populations. School faculty and staff have said that her findings are simply good teaching practices, to which she replied by asking why these practices are so infrequent in classrooms of African American students (Ladson-Billings, 1995, p. 159). It is more common for good teaching practices to be demonstrated in classrooms where the teacher can easily identify with the culture of students and their communities: in using books with characters that look like the students, or incorporating examples of films, sports, and songs that are familiar, the teacher can efficiently engage his or her classes. So, what should a teacher do when they are unfamiliar with the cultures of students and their families?

This was a big question for Yvonne to answer when she first started teaching. Through trial and error, she learned that by starting a cheerleading group—something her female students were heavily invested in but was not offered by the school—she was able to bridge one of the gaps between her classroom and the girls' communities. When students' mothers saw how excited the girls were about this new opportunity, they became involved by sewing cheerleading uniforms and participating in bake sale fundraisers. Eventually, after establishing a trusting relationship, the girls' families encouraged them to stay after school for tutoring sessions (to which families were also invited). Yvonne was able to connect their literacy homework to cheerleading: the girls enjoyed the challenge of creating new cheers based on the literary techniques they had learned in class. Together, the girls read and discussed English books in an environment that became more intimate. The cheerleading group evolved into its own family that supported each other in and outside of school.

While cheerleading might not be a strong suit as an extracurricular activity, any school faculty or staff member can still help create or advise a club at school that is important to students and their communities. Ask students what activities they would like to see at their school and offer ways their club or activity could involve their friends and families. Some community events from extracurricular activities/clubs in Lindsay's own experiences include poetry slams, fundraisers, races, and galleries/exhibit events in local public spaces. Students were responsible for making posters and flyers, promoting their event, arranging community guests and activities, and showcasing their work. Regardless of the event collaboratively chosen, in the process of its development, teachers are certain to help students build their literacy skills while simultaneously building community.

Uniting Families and Classrooms with Literacy Events

When Yvonne first became a teacher, she was working at a school where "parents and community working together with their children's school was a closed door that I knew I had to try and open." Members of the school were not usually inclined to involve themselves in the community, and families did not have avenues by which they could express ideas about their children's education. However, when Yvonne demonstrated how much she cared for her students outside of school grounds, the community stepped up to help her build a literacy space in which everyone could take pride. While the previous sections of this chapter addressed ways to build connections with families outside of the classroom, there are ways to build relationships through literacy events at school as well. These events offer students' family members meaningful roles beyond "classroom helpers" or as attendees at parent–teacher conferences: the goal is to shy away from traditional relationships that prioritize the school's wants and needs and gravitate toward a literacy partnership that demonstrates a genuine student-centered approach.

A Note of Caution

It is tempting to promote engagement by having parents and families volunteer in the classroom. It might even seem like a win-win situation: it is fairly easy to organize, teachers have additional adults for support, parents can see and experience firsthand their children's work, and children have the added benefit of demonstrating what they are learning with their families present. The students might even behave better (this was the case when my mother showed up in school!). However, it is important to remember that the role of volunteers is intended to fulfill the needs of the teacher and/or the classroom, not necessarily the needs of the students (Pushor, 2010).

Additionally, there is new evidence that indicates typical parental involvement in the classroom has a negligible effect on students' performance in school. Prompted by Domina's (2005) research, Gibbs et al. (2021) re-examined traditional measures of parental involvement; their findings suggest "the positive effects of parental involvement are only marginal when measures of parent socioeconomic status and the child's prior skills are accounted for" (p. 2). Furthermore, Robinson and Harris's study (2013) found that "the majority of standard measures of parental involvement in schools are not statistically significant predictors of math and reading skills" (Gibbs et al., 2021, p. 2). It is also crucial to note that, in traditional volunteer positions, families who speak a language that differs from the teacher's might be hesitant to participate for a variety of substantial underlying factors—not for lack of concern, as a teacher in a deficit thinking model might suspect. From her own experience, Yvonne explained,

> Many moms remained hesitant in volunteering because they had never done this before. No one had ever valued their input in their child's education. Parents, especially moms, became a shadow in our school hallways because they did not value their [own input] due to their lack of education or not speaking English.

So, what *is* a good solution to get parents and families involved at school? The following sections offer new or improved ways to replace the outdated approach to engaging families in the literacy classroom.

Community Guest Speakers or Readers

One way to bring the "real world" into the classroom is to invite members of the students' communities to come to talk to the students about literacy-related topics. Ask students about people they interact with every day or on a regular basis: these people are impactful outside of school, so their presence in school will be exciting and meaningful. Students will want to listen to what guests have to say! If you find that students have strong ties to the local YMCA, have a YMCA employee come in and talk about how they use literacy in their everyday lives: creating flyers, communicating with clients and prospective members, researching the latest exercise programs that are trending, for examples. A teacher or administrative staff might even be able to arrange for the community member to collaborate with students to accomplish a real-world task (make a flyer, draft an email to members, create an ad for social media, etc.), resulting in a final product for authentic audiences.

Another option is to work with students' family members to develop a schedule for classroom "Read Aloud" events. Read Aloud programs in schools are not new, but the benefits of adults reading aloud to children are plentiful (van Kleeck et al., 2003). Students are afforded the opportunity to learn new vocabulary, listen to engaging stories, and converse about the texts with people they care about. During each visit, a student's family member reads a book to the class and prefaces their reading with why they picked the book. These guests are encouraged to engage in dialogue with students about the book, from student-created questions about plot to speaker-generated questions about what students think ("Why do you think the boy does not want to go to the baseball game?"). Practicing conversations about literacy in the classroom can often transfer to conversations at home.

When considering the needs of bilingual or multilingual students, inviting their families to read (and to listen to students read) in the classroom allows them access to resources available at school, including free texts or manipulatives to take home to promote home literacy with their children (Rogoff et al., 2015). Throughout her years of teaching, Yvonne had a daily open-door policy for parents to come

and listen to the students ~~read in their home language and read to the~~
students in their home language and the classroom language. Some
family members came daily during reading time to work with students and lead the guided reading center. The classroom experiences
intentionally encouraged families to incorporate these reading activities at home as well.

With a focus on inclusivity, it is necessary to be mindful of book
selection: books should reflect interests, experiences, characters, and
ideas that are relevant to students. This is often problematic for children of color: Meier (2015) reported that culturally relevant literature
is limited in many schools, especially for Black males, which contributes to stereotyping and the struggle for students of color to identify
with protagonists. One way to address this issue during Read Aloud
is to provide a list of book choices for family guest speakers that
feature characters of color, or characters that are positively representative of marginalized populations. Another option is to talk with students' families about books they might like to read that incorporate or
highlight the out-of-school experiences of students. Read these titles
ahead of time and formulate some questions that a classroom teacher
or their guest speakers can ask students during Read Aloud. Both students and families alike will look forward to these events.

Book Tastings

Beverage tastings at restaurants are a popular activity that allows
adults to sample flavors that may appeal to their taste buds: why not
transform the classroom into a venue for book tasting, where students
can sample amazing stories? Book tasting events can offer students
and their families a casual "taste" of the literature options available
to them. Hamilton (2012) noted that "book tasting has been extremely successful in pairing up students with texts that speak to their interests...students [have] room for choice, discovery, and exploration
without any organizational structures that [are] overly fussy or complicated" (p. 17). Encouraging students to bring their family members
provides another way to build literacy connections between the classroom and families as well as students and families. Just as importantly, teachers might spark interest in books that students might never
choose for themselves.

Teachers can start by creating "menus" of books they believe would be interesting and culturally relevant for their students: again, there is tremendous emphasis on knowing students' backgrounds to make authentic connections. Students and their family members can review the menus together, which may be grouped by book genres, protagonists (e.g., female, Latinx, African American), or topics. These book groupings could then be set up at different tables, allowing students to choose from a variety of their interests. Some teachers establish a casual restaurant ambiance by covering tables in tablecloths, placemats, or floral arrangements: imagination is the limit. Set a timer for 10 minutes, or enough time to ensure that students can explore a couple of pages from each group's literary offerings. When the timer goes off, play music to indicate that students and their families should transition to the next table. When all of the transitions are completed, students will be able to "check out" any books of interest from the tasting. If possible, offer several copies of books so that other students or family members can join in on the reading, too.

Engagement of Families Who Speak Different Languages

This section of the chapter is particularly prevalent in today's evolving educational landscape, which is growing more reflective of the cultural, social, and linguistic diversity of our world. As an expert in the field of bilingual education—through personal experience as a student *and* educator—Yvonne offers her valuable insight and research-backed strategies for the specific ways teachers of literacy can engage families who speak different languages.

Our world experiences education in multilingual contexts that denote the importance of recognizing, embracing, and celebrating students and families who speak different languages in and out of the classroom (García, 2011; García & Woodley, 2014). Most importantly, to engage learners who speak different languages, teachers must rely on quality "authentic" and original texts (not just translations) that reflect the students' backgrounds, multiculturalism, and realities in their lives in different languages. Gibbons and Cummins (2002) pointed out that "'learn to read texts' are more challenging to read than an 'authentic' complete story text because it is difficult to predict what comes next, forcing students to rely on cues that are not about reading" (p. 354). An excellent tool that teachers can take advantage of is the rich technology of the Internet, which offers a handful of resources that share full texts in multiple languages. It is also possible to explore with students new literature that goes beyond the nationally-produced texts often provided by school districts. For students and families who speak different languages, teachers need to select books with specific characteristics, such as Spanish to English translations, clear print and illustrations, and repetitive language, with plots that develop into collective, eventful stories.

Yvonne worked with her fifth-grade students pre-selecting the Spanish and English texts, including the vital elements mentioned above, to provide a wide range of topics discussed with her students and families in the classroom library. During open house and after-school pláticas (conversations) with classroom families, teachers can intentionally prompt them on topics of interest and find books to have available for families to select from in the classroom. Families can ask the school librarian to order texts if funds are available. If no funds are available, families can collaborate with teachers and faculty to conduct a community fundraiser, with the goal of enhancing the school (or classroom) library with multicultural and linguistically diverse literature that represents the population of students, families, and the community. Family and community input can assist in identifying meaningful content and relevant instruction as it relates to students.

Biliteracy and Bilingualism

To help bilingual students and families with literacy development, students should have frequent opportunities to read and write in their native language as well as the language utilized in school. According to Au (2006), students should

> [...] engage in the complete processes of reading and writing the standard language according to sociocultural norms and study parts of reading and writing in the standard language. In addition, however, it is necessary to incorporate the literacy practices that the children bring from home. (pp. 363–364)

It is vital to recognize and validate students who speak different languages so that they do not become discouraged in developing their literacy skills in one language or the other. Teachers can do this by understanding and appreciating what it means to be bilingual and biliterate. Biliteracy, as defined by Perez and Torres-Guzman (1996), is "the acquisition and learning of the decoding and encoding of and around print using two linguistic and cultural systems in order to convey messages in a variety of contexts" (p. 54). Knowing how to support students and families in these processes will ultimately contribute to students' development of literacy skills.

Strategies to Support Multilingual Students and Families

Families of students who speak different languages rely on various print and non-print resources and practices implemented in their homes and communities with goals to support their children's language and literacy. Valuable resources and practices that can be used at home for literacy practice have been researched extensively; they include:

> [...] puzzles, videos as didactic tools, singing when the child has difficulty learning a concept (e.g., singing multiples of the number 10), teaching the names of colors while watching television, engaging in interactive games while in costume, and having the child deliver a speech to the family. (Bridges et al., 2015, pp. 259–279)

Additional literacy learning resources and practices include

> [...] playing a number/lottery game, using a flipchart at home to write, using play dough to form letters, writing letters on a chalkboard wall, using an Internet-connected computer to explain words through pictures and video, and reading books from their home or community library. (Bridges et al., 2015, p. 181)

It is imperative to select strategies based on students' specific needs, skill levels, and available resources.

Ada (2003) reminded us that poetry, song, and folklore are essential in reading practices. Converting texts to songs or poems—and using songs, poetry, or folklore as core texts for analysis—may help students retain information about the literature and practice the skills used to decode it. It is also helpful to draw from literature written in two or more languages, as well as other multicultural texts that complement students' backgrounds, cultures, and experiences. Some additional home literacy strategies and activities that may benefit bi-literacy development for students who speak different languages are outlined below.

Literature Circles

Literature circles can be effective for any type of text, language, topic, content area, or age group. Selecting texts in multiple languages (the languages students use at home and at school) is a simple way to demonstrate that teachers care about *all* students' literacy growth and development. It promotes a deeper understanding of a text in two languages instead of one while ensuring that students who are learning a second language have an opportunity to fully grasp the content just as much as students who know the standard classroom language. Literature circles are defined as "small heterogeneous groups in which students all read the same story and each student contributes unique information about the story through an assigned responsibility" (Barone & Barone, 2016, p. 69). Some example responsibilities might be to illustrate a scene from the text, explain the plot, or identify unfamiliar vocabulary words. Teachers should know students' strengths and weaknesses prior to grouping and assigning responsibilities to students.

While literature circles must be carefully orchestrated in school, it is a great idea to extend this practice to families as well, where they can be more casual and intimate. Yvonne incorporated literature circles in her classroom and invited families to participate in them as well. One year, one of Yvonne's students shared that his extended family had come to visit them from Mexico and brought Spanish texts as gifts. Her student, Mario, suggested that his family form a literature circle to read the text aloud and stop to discuss the storyline. Mario even mentioned that they started sharing moments in their personal life that connected them to the story they were reading.

Readers Theater and Literary Performances

Yvonne also recommends the implementation of Readers Theater, in which students put on live performances that convey the plot of a text to an authentic audience. Live performances may include a karaoke or musical-type event (singing a text), a dramatic reenactment, a puppet show, or a poetry slam. Regardless of the theatrical mode, there is evidence that Readers Theater has a large, positive effect on word recognition automaticity and reading prosody (Young & Rasinski, 2018). This is due to the frequent repetition or repeated readings of a text as students learn their lines. Offer texts that are written in two languages, which may be sung in canon or read in alternating patterns. If a teacher is unable to use a multilingual text, consider integrating phrases or words from students' native language that are essential to the text. *All* students can build their literacy skills in two languages with these strategies.

Additionally, Readers Theater builds unity among classmates as they collaborate to perform a production, even if some students struggle with the text. Young and Rasinski (2018) posited that "Readers Theater (and perhaps other similar activities) possesses several elements that increase not only reading fluency, but also other often neglected and unassessed individual differences in reading such as motivation, confidence and reading self-efficacy" (p.478) as a result of students reading and working together. In terms of their "authentic audience," this should stretch beyond the classroom teacher and school community. Other classes and educators may benefit from viewing students' Readers Theater performances but also consider what makes an audience "authentic" for students. When possible, invite families and community members to view the performances and make suggestions for Readers Theater texts. They may even want to get involved in cameo roles, serve as a collaborating artist for a lyrical or poetic performance, and offer their time to build a set or play a musical accompaniment.

Summary

In conclusion, the first step of supporting students and engaging families in student literacy development is to adjust one's teaching mindset to reflect the needs, values, backgrounds, and experiences of *students*. It is detrimental to hold onto literacy practices, materials, and lessons that the teacher enjoys or believes are "right" if they compromise students' abilities to learn. The next step is to truly get to know students and their families, which can be accomplished in multiple ways: phone calls, home or in-person visits (off campus), and virtual meetings. Making an effort to know what is important to students outside of school will help build relationships that transfer into the classroom. Conversations with families need to be exactly that—opportunities to promote two-way communication, which ensure that teachers are making their intentions clear and that families can voice their ideas or concerns. This process can alleviate anxiety or uncertainty for both parties. Additionally, offering take-home resources, such as literacy bags and bilingual literature, can help build a direct connection from the classroom to home.

Go a step further and bring engaging community figures to class! They might be very willing and excited to read to students or share aspects of their lives that incorporate literacy. Inviting families to participate in meaningful (not just subservient) roles, discussions, and events in the classroom can promote home conversations about literacy. Lastly, celebrate bilingualism in the classroom by integrating the home languages of students in various ways, from book selections in literature circles to culturally based folklore as the premise of readers' theater.

Teaching literacy is work that extends far beyond the classroom. The practices suggested within this chapter are intended to help professional learners develop their skills in building and maintaining literacy-focused relationships with students' families. It is the authors' hope that their research and experiences will inform the curriculum and instruction of many professional learners invested in meaningful literacy development for all students.

References

Ada, A. F. (2003). *A magical encounter: Latino children's literature in the classroom*. Allyn & Bacon/Longman Publishers.

Au, K.H. (2006). Diversity, technology, and the literacy achievement gap. In M.C. McKenna, L.D. Labbo, R.D. Kieffer, & D. Reinking (Eds.), *International handbook of literacy and technology* (Vol. 2, pp. 363–367). Erlbaum.

Barone, D., & Barone, R. (2016). "Really," "Not possible," "I can't believe it": Exploring informational text in literature circles. *The Reading Teacher, 70*(1), 69–81. https://doi.org/10.1002/trtr.1472

Brand, S. T., Marchand, J., Lilly, E., & Child, M. (2014). Home–school literacy bags for twenty-first-century preschoolers. *Early Childhood Education Journal, 42*(3), 163–170.

Bridges, M., Cohen, S. R., Scott, L., Fuller, B., Anguiano, R., Figueroa, A. M., & Livas-Dlott, A. (2015). Home activities of Mexican American children: Structuring early socialization and cognitive engagement. *Cultural Diversity and Ethnic Minority Psychology, 21*(2), 181–190.https://doi.org/10.1007/s10643-013-0603-8

Daniels, H. (2006). What's the next big thing with literature circles? *Voices From the Middle, 13*(4), 10–15.

Dewey, J. (2001). *The school and society &the child and the curriculum*. University of Chicago Press. (Original work published 1915).

Domina, T. 2005. Leveling the home advantage: Assessing the effectiveness of parental involvement in elementary school. *Sociology of Education,78*(3), 233–249.https://doi.org/10.1177%2F003804070507800303

Ferlazzo, L., & Hammond, L. A. (2009). *Building parent engagement in schools*. Linworth Publishing.

García, O. (2011). *Bilingual education in the 21st century: A global perspective*. John Wiley & Sons.

García, O., & Woodley, H. H. (2014). Bilingual education. In M. Bigelow, &J. Ennser-Kananen (Eds.), *The Routledge handbook of educational linguistics* (pp. 154–166). Routledge.

García, S., & Guerra, P. (2004). Deconstructing deficit thinking: Working with educators to create more equitable learning environments. *Education and Urban Society, 36*(2), 150–168.https://doi.org/10.1177/0013124503261322

Gibbons, P., & Cummins, J. (2002). *Scaffolding language, scaffolding learning: Teaching second language learners in the mainstream classroom*. Heinemann.

Gibbs, B. G., Marsala, M., Gibby, A., Clark, M., Alder, C., Hurst, B., Steinacker, D., & Hutchison, B. (2021). "Involved is an interesting word": An empirical case for redefining school-based parental involvement as parental efficacy. *Social Sciences, 10*(5), 156. https://doi.org/10.3390/socsci10050156

Gonzalez, J. E., Bengochea, A., Justice, L., Yeomans-Maldonado, G., & McCormick, A. (2019). Native Mexican parents' beliefs about children's literacy and language development: A mixed-methods study. *Early Education and Development, 30*(2), 259–279.https://doi.org/10.1080/10409289.2018.1542889

Goodall, J. (2018). Learning-centred parental engagement: Freire reimagined. *Educational Review, 70*(5), 603–621.https://doi.org/10.1080/00131911.2017.1358697

Hamilton, B. J. (2012). Cultivating reading interest with book tasting. *School Library Monthly, 29*(3), 17–19.

Heinrichs, J. (2015). Teachers and parents: Learning from each other through home visits. *LEARNing Landscapes, 8*(2), 213–228. https://doi.org/10.36510/learnland.v8i2.705

Ladson-Billings, G. (1994). *The dreamkeepers*. Jossey-Bass Publishing Co.

Ladson-Billings, G. (1995). But that's just good teaching! The case for culturally relevant pedagogy. *Theory Into Practice, 34*(3), 159–165. http://www.jstor.org/stable/1476635

Leavitt-Noble, K. A., & Grande, M. (2012). Creating school-to-home literacy bags. *New Teacher Advocate, 20*(1), 10–11.

Meier, T. (2015). "The brown face of hope": Reading engagement and African American boys. *The Reading Teacher, 68*(5), 335– 343. https://doi.org/10.1002/trtr.1310

Miller Marsh, M., & Turner-Vorbeck, T. (2010). *(Mis)understanding families: Learning from real families in our schools*. Teachers College Press.

Moll, L. C., Amanti, C., Neff, D., & Gonzalez, N. (1992). Funds of knowledge for teaching: Using a qualitative approach to connect homes and classrooms. *Theory Into Practice, 31*(2), 132–141.

Perez, B., & Torres-Guzmán, M. E. (1996). *Learning in two worlds: An integrated Spanish/English biliteracy approach*. Longman Publishing Group.

Pushor, D. (2010). Are schools doing enough to learn about families? In M. Miller Marsh, & T. Turner-Vorbeck (Eds.), *(Mis)understanding families: Learning from real families in our schools* (pp. 4–16). Teachers College Press.

Richardson, M. V., Miller, M. B., Richardson, J. A., & Sacks, M. K. (2008). Literacy bags to encourage family involvement. *Reading Improvement, 45*(1), 3.

Robinson, K., & Harris, A.L. 2013. *The broken compass.* Harvard University Press.

Rogoff, B., Mejía-Arauz, R., & Correa-Chávez, M. (2015). A cultural paradigm—Learning by observing and pitching in. In M. Correa-Chavez, R. Mejia-Arauz, & B. Rogoff (Eds.), *Advances in child development and behavior* (Vol. 49, pp. 1–22).Academic Press.

van Kleeck, A., Stahl, S., & Bauer, E. (2003). *On reading books to children: Parents and teachers.* Erlbaum.

Young, C., & Rasinski, T. (2018). Readers theatre: Effects on word recognition automaticity and reading prosody. *Journal of Research in Reading, 41*(3), 475–485. https://doi.org/10.1111/1467-9817.12120

Chapter 5

Multimodal Literacies for English Language Learners

Cesar Riojas, Ph.D.

Abstract

As the digital age of K-12 instruction expands, educators working with English Language Learners (ELLs) have the ability to use multimodal literacies to engage and find meaningful connections with their students. Multimodal literacy professional learning strategies, when implemented correctly, utilize students' prior knowledge and experiences to create a positive and welcoming classroom environment. This chapter will provide examples from my own personal teaching experiences with multimodal literacy strategies and how they can easily be implemented into your classroom. With an understanding that teaching and technology can be seamlessly melded, this chapter will identify how certain occasions to improve ELL fluency may not only come through spoken or written language but through the use of digital platforms.

Introduction

As an educator along the United States/Mexico border, I have had my fair share of English Language Learners (ELLs) in my classroom. The majority of my students are of Hispanic descent, and a portion of those children live in Mexico and cross the border daily for schooling. It is an absolute pleasure to live and work in an area where the Southern United States and Northern Mexico blend languages and customs together to create a new cultural region filled with the best of the two nations. This blending does require me, as an educator, to really reflect on the academic success of the students at my campus in a new light. There is a balance that must be held in schools where cultures mix (Medin & Bang, 2013). It is our responsibility to give our best efforts to encourage these students to continue their rich cultural heritage while connecting with them in a way that helps them excel academically (Smith & Smith, 2008). Therefore, how can I support my students to gain the academic language and skills needed to pass my class and the end-of-year assessments? Most of my students do not speak English at home or with their friends, so the only time they hear the language is in the classroom. I needed my students to practice their English skills and challenge them academically.

The most frustrating part of being an educator is sitting through professional development that is not applicable or tailored to your own needs as a teacher. In this chapter, I will share practical uses of multi-modal literacy strategies that I have used in my own classroom that both new and veteran can apply to their classrooms. These various multimodal literacy professional learning strategies will help educators develop activities and create a digitally cultured environment where all students can feel connected (Berger & Foster, 2020). With the merging of teaching and technology, I will also identify different occasions wherein the fluency of ELLs may be enhanced through spoken or written language and through the use of digital platforms.

What is Multimodal Literacy?

Multimodal literacy is the use of semiotic resources and modalities; and, at the same time, makes meaning of the linguistic and visual choices used to convey information and ideas (O'Halloran & Lim, 2011). Digital media facilitates the creation of multimodal texts that combine writing, image, sounds, and other modes, which can be easily shared through a computer, cell phone, or any electronic device (Gee, 2004). Society has evolved to become dependent on the use of technology to complete even the smallest of tasks. Communication has evolved from traditional face-to-face conversations to communicating through a screen (Hafner, 2014). Students are now reading, writing, and communicating through social media while leaving educators concerned as it relates to literacy practices in the written mode.

A different audience, purpose, and medium are all factors that have the potential to shape the way that a written message is created and interpreted (Hafner, 2014). Multimodal literacy and communication are happening outside of the classroom, so it is up to the educator to find a way to connect with students. Multimodal literacies have given the opportunity to students who were unable to speak and write a language to convey their message (Sewell & Denton, 2011). The internet, mobile devices, and other digital media have given educators a way of connecting with students in a way that was not possible in years prior.

Why Use Multimodal Literacy in the Classroom?

The first step in furthering your understanding of multi-modal literacies is to utilize one that you are already familiar with. As an educator, you challenge yourself to learn about something that is difficult, but there are various digital tools that are user-friendly and easy to adapt (Crawford Camiciottoli & Campoy-Cubillo, 2018). All it takes is the right attitude to embrace these tools and practice using them. Moreover, there are multiple reasons why digital literacy techniques are a great tool for ELL students. Learning can often be perceived as boring and frustrating. However, students that are provided color, sound, and engaging activities are more likely to experience positive outcomes in the classroom (Yi, 2014). ELL students are able to take activities that would normally be challenging and engage with these tools in the classroom. Technology can also be used to explain difficult concepts (e.g., visual images in lieu of text) that would otherwise be challenging for ELL students due to the language barrier (Pandya, 2012). As ELL students are struggling with their second language, these technologies can definitely bridge the gap between what the students know and what they need to learn.

Accessibility is another valuable feature of multimodal literacies (Tungka, 2018). In the past, technology in the classroom was a luxury only certain districts could afford. Now, most classrooms are equipped with either laptops, Chromebooks, iPads, tablets, and the majority of students carry a cell phone in the secondary level. There are free applications with built-in videos and games that I will introduce throughout the chapter.

Not to be forgotten is the idea that in digital platforms, students are learning at their own pace. The process of learning a new language is often strenuous and frustrating (Cumming et al., 2012). With only themselves as competition, the student can truly focus on self-improvement. This process is even more frustrating when you are surrounded by peers who are unable to communicate with you. From my own experience, I learned that apps, digital comics, and video games are an excellent way for students to express themselves, particularly if they are not fluent in English. By responding to questions, posting images, text, and even videos, students can freely express themselves without embarrassment. Overall, learning becomes a fun process when digital tools are utilized to help ELLs.

Multimodal Literacy Professional Learning Strategies

There is a certain unpredictability to teaching, not knowing who is going to walk in your classroom door. Every year, every week, every day, every class period is a new adventure. At any moment, a school counselor can knock on your door and say, "You have a new student; he is new to this country so have a little patience with him." These very words have been said to me on multiple occasions. I already had my scope and sequence, and my lesson plans perfectly planned out. I knew how fast my students were grasping the concepts, so I was aware of how long each lesson would take and how much time was needed for my students to complete their assignments. Nevertheless, none of these included students who did not know the language. I needed to find a way that incorporated their prior knowledge, their very limited English language skills, and their interests; and then somehow tie it into my history lessons.

I have put together a list of multimodal literacy strategies I have utilized or have seen used by coworkers over the years with ELL students that have been successful. In the past, I was hesitant to use multi-modal strategies in the classroom because I thought students would be easily distracted and would have a hard time staying on task. I had heard stories from other teachers about their disastrous attempts to use iPads in the classroom. However, I quickly learned that in any lesson, the outcome is usually determined by the teacher's preparation.

Blended Learning

It is important to realize that multimodal teaching does not take the place of traditional classroom techniques. Teachers still need to actively monitor student engagement, plan lessons effectively, and deliver an engaging lesson regardless of the technology being utilized or not. When we have English Language Learners in the classroom, it is important to find a balance between teaching the content as well as teaching our students the basics of the English language. At the end of the day, if we focus on content, our ELL students will be behind, and if we slow down our lessons, our English-speaking students will suffer. This is where blended learning plays an important role in our classrooms. Boelens et al. (2018) describe blended learning as the art of brewing technology with the traditional methods of education.

Putting Blended Learning into Practice

During the COVID-19 lockdowns, educators and students were thrust into a new age of using online platforms to learn and teach. At that point, we all had to become Google Classroom experts. We had to learn how to create a classroom, how to send invitation links to students, how to upload lessons, and how to upload media. Everything at our campus had to be online where our students had 24/7 access. During that time, teachers noticed students turning in assignments at all hours of the day. Some would turn in the assignments early in the morning, after lunch, or even in the wee hours of the morning.

A helpful feature of using Google Classroom is that it lets the instructor know how long students have been working on an assignment. Some students completed assignments within five minutes, and others would take close to an hour. Notably, the ELL students at my campus were completing the assignments at a much slower rate but still turning them in on time. When students work at their own pace, there is less pressure to complete assignments because they are not conscious of watching their classmates turn in their assignments. They can take their time and really think about the questions before answering. They have the ability to use dictionary.com to look up words, do a Google search, and translate any word (e.g., Spanish to English). Google Classroom gave ELL students the opportunity to take control of their education.

Google Classroom was a great tool when teachers and students work from home, but it can be a great asset when students return to campus. Incorporating Google Classroom as part of the lesson gives teachers the opportunity to have students complete assignments, take quizzes, and research at home. It can even free up time in your classroom for more discussions, group activities (e.g., debates), or any lesson that may not fit in your scope and sequence due to time constraints. The flexibility to have more group work also increases the communication skills of my ELL students. Whether they are talking English or Spanish, they are communicating and having discussions about the lesson, expanding their vocabulary, and building social skills.

Online Game-Based Learning Platforms

Game-based learning is an excellent way to engage students in the classroom and allow ELL students to associate sentences, words, and phrases with associated graphics. Thanks to content creators, there are now multiple platforms that are tailored for different age groups (Beavis, 2014). There are also content-specific categories catering to elementary and secondary school-aged children. For ELL students, there are games tailored to support their own mastery of skills concepts. The use of these types of games can also increase ELL students' ease of mind. Playing with friends and peers can reduce their anxiety about learning and speaking English (Hur & Suh, 2012). In addition, online games can allow these students to integrate visually and digitally with different learning domains, such as reading, writing, speaking, and listening, while also learning new concepts. The beauty of online educational video games is that students immerse themselves in the game without even realizing they are learning concepts. They are critically reading and thinking during the entire process of playing and are just having fun. Moreover, when interacting within the online game-based platform, students are often allowed a certain level of anonymity, allowing them to make mistakes without the fear of judgment.

Putting Online Game-Based Learning Platforms into Practice

A question you may ponder is, "how can I incorporate video games into my lesson?" Let me explain how I have used game-based learning platforms in my classroom. As a history teacher, I try my best to incorporate images, maps, videos, and other media that can make my lesson meaningful. However, reading and writing are necessary, regardless of the subject. Every one of my lessons included reading passages, reading maps, writing, and introducing content-related vocabulary.

As my students entered my classroom, they would pick an entry ticket. This ticket was a question about the previous day's lesson, and it was formatted similar to the end-of-the-year assessment. I would give them a couple of minutes to answer the question and then discuss the answers as a class. This is where I would quickly learn if I would need to reteach yesterday's lesson or move on. However, I noticed a pattern emerging from my ELL students. They refused to discuss their entry ticket question. I had always assumed they were shy or embarrassed because they were still learning the English language and did not feel comfortable expressing themselves aloud. After speaking to several of my ELL students in confidence regarding their lack of participation, it became apparent that they did not understand the entry ticket questions. They understood the previous day's lesson but were confused with words and phrases such as "read the excerpt," "which of the following prompted," "what is the significance," and "compare and contrast." I was taken aback upon hearing these confusions from my students. Nowhere in my scope and sequence and in my lesson plans had I included non-academic vocabulary words—words that I assumed all my students should know by the eighth grade.

Quickly, I needed to find a way that I could teach my content as well as teach the needed vocabulary to understand the end-of-the-year assessment questions. I thought of a game I could customize to the specific needs of my ELL students. I found Kahoot and Quizlet to be very useful in this circumstance. I could create questions, and my students could freely answer without feeling judged by their classmates. My ELL students could not get enough of these two games. The competitive side of all my students emerged, and at the same time, my ELL students were learning new vocabulary, reading at ease, reviewing academic content, as well as thinking critically. When learning became a competition with Kahoot, my ELL students were asking questions about the meaning of words I thought they would never ask aloud in the classroom.

Language Learner Apps

An excellent method to increase ELL students' language integration in the classroom is through the use of English language learning apps. These apps make learning extremely accessible because students can have them on their phones and use them throughout the day, even at home. For example, I discovered that Busuu is a fun and interactive way to learn any language. This app allows students to learn English in context and help them with conversational English as well as review content vocabulary. Language learner apps expose the students to pronunciations, sentence structures, and vocabulary skills needed for language acquisition.

Putting Language Learner Apps into Practice

Many students in my area, particularly daily border crossers, rarely find opportunities to use English outside of the school setting. Daily practice is one of the best ways to feel comfortable with a new language. So, as part of my daily lessons, I would assign Busuu activities to my ELL students. I found that using the app produced more daily engagement than traditional writing assignments. The benefit to using Busuu is that I was able to monitor my students' performance on the app through my teacher account, check student log-in attempts, completed activities, and provide feedback.

Digital Word Walls

Digital word walls are tools that can be shared graphically on a projector throughout the day. Digital word walls can be placed on iPads or computers. They allow students to visualize root words, meanings, sentence examples, and images throughout the day (Sewell & Denton, 2011). This process can increase their understanding of the English language, as well as increase their connection to their school and classmates. Most programs are also able to have the words and definitions read to them. The daily use of digital word walls will familiarize students with the vocabulary needed for conversational language as well as an academic language.

Putting Digital Word Walls into Practice

Not only are digital word walls a convenient place to store a year's worth of vocabulary, but it is also easy to set up. While doing classroom observations, I was introduced to digital word walls. I was amazed by its accessibility and ease of use, so I started a digital word wall. On Google Slides, teachers have the ability to create a slide for every vocabulary term used throughout the year. I have seen digital world walls with pictures, videos, and attached links to each term. I thought my ELL students can get a better understanding of vocabulary words if they were constantly visible. Digital word walls can also be utilized as a review activity for any approaching quizzes.

Throughout my teaching career, I was taught that we should always have a word wall somewhere in our classroom so students can always see the vocabulary taught in the classroom. Yet, my word walls were always placed on one side of the classroom. I had to change them every six weeks because of the new vocabulary and content presented throughout those weeks. So, in reality, the words on my word wall would be placed on my bulletin board and then be forgotten the following six weeks.

Digital Storytelling

Digital storytelling is one of the advancements in the digital classroom's instructional design and is becoming a promising transformative technology-supported approach for enhancing learning (Yang & Wu, 2012). Each digital story challenges students to carefully select edit images, videos, and audio from personal collections to other multimedia resources that support the story and learning goals, thereby developing technology and media skill (EDUCAUSE Learning Initiative, 2007). Communication-based activities can greatly aid ELL students' English language proficiency in the classroom while engaging with their peers. There are multiple online resources that allow for the creation of stories. As an educator, you may need to get creative with this approach while also creating a platform that furthers social integration between ELL students and their peers.

Putting Digital Storytelling into Practice

An enjoyable way for ELL students to tell a story is by creating their own digital comic. A valuable website for students to create digital comics is Storyboard That! This website allows students to create their own stories using images and text boxes. For example, after my lesson about the American Revolution, I wanted my students to create a comic with a contemporary twist. Creating digital comics gave my students an opportunity to demonstrate their understanding of the lesson. They were immediately drawn to the Storyboard That! website because it was a creative outlet to relate their own understanding of the lesson. My ELL students particularly enjoyed it because it allowed them to tell their own version of the story using as many of the related English words as they knew.

Virtual Field Trips

Virtual field trips can be an excellent way to immerse your ELL students in local and national culture. There are multiple virtual field trips offered through government-sponsored websites. Educators can use virtual field trips in combination with class activities and games. Examples of virtual field trips are The White House, Mount Rushmore, the Statue of Liberty, the Grand Canyon, and Yosemite National Park. Virtual field trips can also be organized according to the topic of the classroom. For example, if learning about animals, there are virtual trips to zoos. For example, the San Diego Zoo has a live option that allows students to engage with animals and zookeepers. This approach provides the student with a unique opportunity to learn about animals and words associated with specific animals.

Putting Virtual Field Trips into Practice

When someone from out of town, state, or country enters my classroom, I try my best to make them feel welcome and accepted. Their classmates enjoy hearing about other places and comparing their own traditions with new students. I have had several students from Southern Mexico and Central America enter my classroom. The majority of my students had never been to the area, and my new students were English Language Learners, so it was hard for them to communicate. I found the website, AirPano, which gives stunning videos and photography of different parts of the world. Once I display videos and images of the incoming students' home country or places they have traveled, my students would become very animated. They also want to tell the class about life back home in their native country. Simple activities like virtual field trips can make a student feel welcome, and it helps the rest of the class appreciate another culture.

ELL Teacher Networks

One of the best ways to improve your multimodal literacy professional learning strategy is to engage with other teachers. The use of ELL teacher networks, such as the ones found in Facebook and other online forums, can provide teachers with the connection with other teachers teaching in the same grade level and who also might have similar concerns. With teacher networks, you can discuss techniques that have worked not worked, as well as present specific questions. As mentioned earlier, ELL students can come from different backgrounds. Accordingly, you may need to seek sources that are specific to their culture. By connecting with other teachers, you are able to apply the best practices that were suggested by other teachers. For instance, social media groups are a valuable resource because you can ask a question, and teachers all over the country may share their own struggles and give you possible solutions to your specific issue. In most cases, a teacher simply needs other perspectives to consider and other ideas to try in their classrooms.

Summary

There are a variety of resources online that provide an extension of online learning through a purchasable curriculum tailored to the needs of ELL students. The curriculum required for digital competencies for ELL students must be engaging and fun. Resources that provide publishable content can be used to create digital activities, lesson plans, and engaging videos. If you are a new educator, there are digital programs that can be purchased by the district for ELL students. Some tools are even free. This can be a wonderful starting point to gain the desired learning competencies through pre-prepared lesson plans. Additionally, these programs offer insight into the specific learning content, skills, and knowledge that is gained in each program. Consequently, you can employ specific content when it is appropriate for your classroom.

Not every one of these multimodal learning strategies may be applicable in your classroom; however, there is a great advantage in learning new digital tools. You can teach them one at a time, and once you have mastered a tool, you may go to the next one, learn it, and so on. There is much to be gained in embracing new ideas and technologies and incorporating them into our lessons. Multimodal literacies could open a new way of communication with our students while emphasizing students' creative development and ideas through a deeper understanding of the content. We must be innovators in teaching by adapting, keeping up with the times, and becoming educational pioneers for a technology-rich classroom.

References

Apperley, T., & Beavis, C. (2013). A model for critical games literacy. *E-Learning and Digital Media, 10*(1).

Beavis, C., (2014). Games as text, games as action: Video games in the English classroom. *Journal of Adolescent & Adult Literacy, 57*(6), 433–439. https://doi.org/10.1002/jaal.275

Berger, W., & Foster, E. (2020). Beautiful questions in the classroom. SAGE Publications.

Boelens, R., Voet, M., & De Wever, B. (2018). The design of blended learning in response to student diversity in higher education: Instructors' views and use of differentiated instruction in blended learning. *Computers and Education, 120*, 197–212. https://doi.org/10.1016/j.compedu.2018.02.009

Crawford Camiciottoli, B., & Campoy-Cubillo, M. C. (2018). Introduction: The nexus of m   multimodality, multimodal literacy, and English language teaching in research and practice in higher education settings. *System (Linköping), 77*, 1–9.

Cumming, J., Kimber, K., & Wyatt-Smith, C. (2012). Enacting policy, curriculum and teacher   conceptualizations of multimodal literacy and English in assessment and accountability. *English in Australia, 47*(1), 9–18.

EDUCAUSE Learning Initiative. (2007). *7 things you should know about digital storytelling.* https://library.educause.edu/-/media/files/library/2007/1/eli7021-pdf.pdf

Gee, J. P. (2004). Situated language and learning: A critique of traditional schooling. Routledge

Hafner, C. (2014). Embedding digital literacies in English language teaching: Students' digital video projects as multimodal ensembles. *TESOL Quarterly, 48*(4), 655–685.

Hur, J., & Suh, S. (2012). Making learning active with interactive whiteboards, podcasts, and digital storytelling in ELL classrooms. *Computers in the Schools, 29*(4), 320–338.

O'Halloran, K. L. & Lim, F. V. (2011). Dimensioner af multimodal literacy. Viden om   laesning. 10, 14-21.

Medin, D., & Bang, M. (2013). Culture in the classroom. *Phi Delta Kappan, 95*(4), 64–67. Pandya, J., (2012). Unpacking pandora's box: Issues in the assessment of English learners' literacy skill development in multimodal classrooms. *Journal of Adolescent & Adult Literacy, 56*(3), 181–185. https://doi.org/10.1002/JAAL.00124

Sewell, W., & Denton, S. (2011). Multimodal Literacies in the Secondary English Classroom.   *The English Journal, 100*(5), 61–65. http://www.jstor.org/stable/23047804

Smith, D., & Smith, B. J. (2008). Urban educators' voices: Understanding culture in the   classroom. *The Urban Review, 41*(4), 334–351.

https://doi.org/10.1007/s11256-008-0108-8

Tungka, N., (2018). Guided literacy instruction: Helping students read multimodal English-   m e d i u m texts. *Indonesian Journal of Applied Linguistics, 8*(2), 345–357.

Yang, Y., & Wu, W.-C. I. (2012). Digital storytelling for enhancing student academic   achievement, critical thinking, and learning motivation: A year-long experimental study.   *Computers and Education, 59*(2), 339–352.

Yi, Y. (2014). Possibilities and challenges of multimodal literacy practices in teaching and learning English as an additional language. *Language and Linguistics Compass, 8*(4), 158-159.https://doi.org/10.1111/lnc3.12076

Chapter 6

Stances for Effective Feedback

Shona Rose, Ph.D.

Abstract

Examining the approach of recruiting, responding to, and delivering feedback refines the processes of a professional learner and their impact on students. This chapter explores how practitioners can abandon corrective stances that harm or do not impact the quality of learner products and performances. In contrast, the collaborative stance allows practitioners to adopt stances that trigger students' awareness of how they have performed, how to make progress, and how to evaluate their next product or performance. Next, the chapter explores the characteristics and impact of each stance on the learner's response. The following characteristics of feedback for each stance are addressed: purposes; focus; questions, directionality, dominance, and feedback types. At the end of each characteristic, key principles are offered to guide the application. The chapter concludes with a description of how each stance triggers a mechanical or a cognitive response from learners and the impact each stance has on the quality of the learner's contributions.

Introduction

As a professional learner, the way you recruit, respond to, and deliver feedback relates directly to developing your instructional expertise as well as the success of the learners you serve. From your own personal experience, you probably know that feedback can beillustrative and helpful, crushing and paralyzing, or useless at worst. Hattie (2009) validates our experiences that feedback is one of the most powerful influencers of student growth. Feedback can also motivate and help persistence through difficulty (Narciss, 2008). When learners use and internalize feedback, the performance improves (William, 2011). Yet, feedback is also the most variable in impact (Dweck, 2007; Hattie, 2009; Hattie, Gan, and Brooks, 2017; Kluger and DeNisi, 1996). Frankly, sometimes feedback works; sometimes it doesn't.

While we know that feedback is supposed to help learning, the presence of it doesn't mean that learners find the feedback effective (Brookhart, 2004; Sadler, 2010) or that it is even used (Carless, 2006). Hattie spurred my thinking with his three feedback questions: "Where am I going?" which represents goals, "How am I going?" which references progress achievement of success criteria, and "Where to next?" which references the next steps in refinement (Hattie, 2009, p.177). But the question remains: What does that look and sound like when I give feedback to my learners?

What *is* it about feedback that causes the impact we wish to see? Most of us have viewed feedback as correction and teaching. However, when teachers in my dissertation study about feedback to writing took a corrective stance, the quality of student writing did not improve. In some instances, student performance declined. Conversely, when teachers took a collaborative stance, the quality of student writing improved in multiple areas—even in areas the teacher never addressed.

Here's why stance matters: each stance causes a reciprocal response from the learner that triggers success or failure. If the teacher is Corrector, the student is Rule-Breaker. If the teacher is Finder-of-Error, the student is Passive Acceptor. If the teacher is The Expert, the student is The Novice.

Instead, as a collaborator, you become a thought partner, awarding the student agency as the primary decision-maker. As the audience, you share how you make meaning with their performance. The collaborator grapples with the concepts *as* a learner. Together, learners *and* teachers think, apply, and create, engaging in meaningful changes to products and thinking processes (Hattie 2009).

Hattie explains that very little of what we do as educators causes harm (2009). He goes on to say that feedback has the most promise as an instructional approach yet is the most variable in effectiveness (2009). Therefore, it has become a moral imperative for me to delineate what I need to *stop* doing as The Corrector and what I need to

~~*start* doing as a collaborator. I challenge you to do the same.~~

In the following sections, I'll share six principles about feedback stances and their impact. First, I'll describe the approach and impact of The Corrector. Then, I'll share practices and the impact of a collaborator. Each section ends with how collaborative stance characteristics improve feedback in general.

Roles as Collaborators and Correctors

When you choose your role for feedback, you also choose the role for the learner. In the first few words of the conferences below, the teacher's stance positions their roles and their students' roles very differently. (Note: I used a researcher's journal to keep my notes and transcripts throughout the dissertation process. S1 represents site one. S1 represents student two, and so on. I named the transcripts by the research activities.)

Excerpt A	Excerpt B
Teacher: You start out once again with one of those valid introduction tips we talked about. You can ask a question that's based on the prompt. Good way to start that out, but I would tell you to remember that the prompt was not about...(Researcher's Journal, S2S3, Initial Conference Transcript, Lines 8-14).	Teacher: What do you think about what you've done so far? I know I sent you a long note almost a week ago, and you responded to it. Student: I think I know what to say, but I can't ever put it into good words. Teacher: That's fair. (Researcher's Journal, S1S1, Initial Conference transcript, Lines 27-37).

Figure One: Feedback Samples

Both teachers had honorable intentions. One approach worked to improve student writing, and one did not. One teacher posed herself as Corrector. The other didn't. As a result, students viewed *themselves* differently, changing their reception of the feedback (Hattie, 2009).

Corrector Roles and Impact

In Excerpt A, feedback originated from The Corrector: the student's only choice was to view themselves as Rule-Breaker. The Corrector pointed out errors while the student passively received criticism. While The Corrector gave both praise and criticism, the student experienced judgement. After a corrective conference, the first two feedback questions have been answered for the student. The student has no answers to resolve the third question: "Where to next?" (Hattie, 2009, p. 177).

Collaborator Roles and Impact

In Excerpt B above, the opening evaluative probe invites the student to think and reflect, naming their own needs and struggles. The collaborator serves as a thought partner, establishing the learner as the lead decision-maker and evaluator. The student's words become feedback *from* the student (Hattie, 2009), which the collaborator uses to paraphrase the student's needs using academic vocabulary. The collaborator names the cognitive actions the learner can use to improve.

In Excerpt B, the collaborator went on to summarize the learner's vague description of struggles: "Because you write it and you are like, 'That's what I meant to say in my head, but [on paper] that's not what I meant?'" (S1S1, Initial Conference, Lines 47-48). After gaining the learner's thoughts, the collaborator could explain how and why the text wasn't working. She continued:

> Teacher: I think that's something I see... I can see that you have your evidence. It's... [pauses to think, tapping the second paragraph] the *evidence* that helps me understand what you are trying to say. Because before, the evidence [points to the introduction] I'm just... 'Where are we going?' *Then* you give me your evidence. I can see how that ties... kind of. I know where you *wanted* to go with that. And if you didn't know what you wanted to say, you wouldn't have been able to pick out evidence that pointed, (Researcher's Journal, S1S1, Initial Conference, Lines 50-57).

The collaborator's words explains 1) how the text impacts her as a meaning maker and audience, 2) pinpoints the location of the problems, and 3) validates the attempt and the learner's evaluation. Because the learner could explain her struggles, the collaborator could then share her transaction with the learner's text (Rosenblatt, 1978). The learner saw how someone else made or struggled to understand their ideas.

Next, I watched the collaborator read aloud to the student. She read exactly what the student had written in the way it was written, wrinkling her nose in accepting confusion and concentration.

Teacher: The system thought they were doing the world *justice* for the *injustice* people of America.

Student: Yeah, that doesn't really make sense.

Teacher: I'm just going to circle that, and we can come back to it.

Teacher: And that's why, when we go into revising, I read my papers out loud. It drives me crazy because I hate to hear the sound of my voice (Researcher's Journal, S1S1, Initial Conference Lines 207-212).

Because of the collaborator's approach, the learner identifies where her writing didn't make sense, pointing out the error and its location.

As such, the collaborator's next comments position herself as a practicing writer and learner: the learner also realizes how the collaborator grapples with the same concepts. After participating in a collaborative conference, the learner can answer all three feedback questions: where they are in reference to the goals, how they are progressing, and a beginning idea of what to do next (Hattie, 2009).

Application. As the collaborator, you follow four principles:

- Principle One: Invite the learner to think with you, evaluating their own learning progress.
- Principle Two: Paraphrase and summarize the learner's thinking using the correct academic terms.
- Principle Three: Read aloud and react to what the learner has said or written. Think aloud to share how you make sense of their performance.
- Principle Four: Position yourself as a learner, naming common struggles, noting how you resolve them.

While the descriptions above come from a writing conference example, several ideas apply to feedback in general. When The Corrector views themselves as the expert grader who points out errors, the learner views themselves as Failure. Conversely, a collaborative approach positions the student as an empowered decision-maker.

Purpose of Feedback

Asking about the purpose of feedback may seem like a moot point: feedback seeks success. Yet, each stance has an unstated purpose and outcome. Corrective purposes lead to compliance and failure, while collaborative purposes build awareness and self-assessment capacity (Fisher, Frey, and Hattie, 2017). Feedback, applied in collaboration, causes growth for both the learner and the teacher. While The Corrector and collaborator look for things to be "correct," our main purpose as a collaborator is growth for all parties. When a learner applies or fails to apply feedback, that response is also data that helps the collaborator refine instructional and feedback techniques to cause growth in the next student performance and instructional act (Hattie, 2009).

Corrective Purposes Lead to Compliance and Failure

Unfortunately, taking the stance as The Corrector results in praise and criticism. Success is praised, which often causes a static mindset and hampers growth (Hattie, 2009). The Rule Breaker receives criticism as judgment. As such, the feedback comes across as a personal indictment, including no useful information for change. Instead of feeling the energy to persist, the learner experiences debilitating judgment about themselves as a person.

I remember another conference with a dyslexic student. During the first conference, the student read what he intended to be there, not what was actually there. The teacher stopped to correct each instance of inaccurate word endings. When the student came to share his revisions, the teacher pointed out that the errors with word endings remained. Frustrated, he threw his pencil down, "I read it over like three times!" (Researcher's Journal, S2S4, Revisions Conference, p. 2). Corrective feedback he received during the conference reminded him of the rules, criteria, and absence of them in his work. The correction did not result in learning how to use word endings in the current paper. As a result, the student judged himself as a Failure. He knew he had not made progress. Yet, The Corrector failed to answer Hattie's (2009) last question: "Where to next?" (p.177). While reading over the paper and looking up words in the dictionary were offered as solutions, these suggestions were not effective solutions for a dyslexic student. In fact, he was unable to realize that he was not making progress in his revision attempt until The Corrector corrected the mistakes again. While he wanted to comply with the Corrector's demands, he simply did not have the ability to do so. The corrective stance placed him where he had begun: Unable.

Collaborative Purposes Build Awareness and Assessment Capability

A collaborative stance builds the student's awareness and capacity for self-assessment that transfers to other contexts (Fisher, Hattie, and Frey, 2018). Let's step into another student's conference. The student felt her thesis statement was not clear.

> Teacher: So I think that it starts weak *here* [points to thesis], so it doesn't help [gestures to bracket the next paragraph] when you get to *this* paragraph. [The teacher then looks at both sides of the paper, scanning for the topics, evidence, and reasons the writer uses in the following paragraphs.]

> Teacher: If we can get two or three reasons used in your paragraphs, we can work that right into this sentence here [brackets the weak thesis] and make a really strong thesis. So I'm going to write that down before we forget [Writes 2-3 reasons], (Researcher's Journal, S1S1, Initial Conference. Lines 111-121).

When the student returned to the revisions conference, she had successfully applied the feedback. We asked the student how she would avoid the problem in the next paper. "I will probably write my draft out like this and just get everything out and then go back to fix the thesis to make sure it connects [touches the thesis] with my evidence [scanning her finger through the following paragraphs] (Researcher's Journal, S1S1, Initial Conference, Lines 365-367; 377-380).

The collaborator gives the learner a focused portion of the performance and allows the student the chance to reflect on how it meets the criteria. When the learner responds, the collaborator probes further to clarify what the learner means. From there, the feedback focuses not on what was right or wrong but the location of strengths and weaknesses and how they might be resolved or improved. In the exchange above, the learner could answer all three of Hattie's (2009) feedback questions: how she was going to do a strong thesis, where and why she needed to make progress, and how she had transferred a specific strategy for writing the next paper.

Note the collaborator's focus on how the learner could write an effective thesis in generalizable terms, regardless of what the topic of the paper was. In essence, the message was not about how to write about the prompt or even how to write a thesis statement. The message was about the process a writer uses to compose: writers review the points in their body paragraphs and use those to reconnect to the thesis, revising both the thesis and body paragraphs when necessary. In other words, the collaboration focuses on the *process* writers use to compose, monitor, and revise their messages in a way a reader can follow. As such, the learner could answer the questions: "Where to next?" *and* how to do so (Hattie, 2009, p. 177).

Notice also that the teacher did not mark the text for a weak thesis. The marks made on the paper pointed out solutions: locations and reminders for revision strategies the learner could use when she revised alone. The best part of this conference was when the student confirmed her learning and writing process. The collaborator knew the learner had mastered the concept and could apply it in a new situation when the topic was something different.

Application. When you adopt a collaborative purpose, you follow four principles:

- Principle One: Help the learner evaluate their own areas of strengths and weaknesses so they can monitor their own path to success.
- Principle Two: Use their performance and the appropriate academic terms to focus on where and how a learner can repair the weaknesses.
- Principle Three: Mark the text or make notes about where the learner could improve by listing solutions. This becomes data the student can use to recall where they should head next.
- Principle Four: Focus on generalizable truths that will help the current performance as well as the next.

The stance we take to our purpose of giving feedback applies to multiple learning contexts. The Corrector praises or criticizes the static, current performance, noting rules, procedures, and criteria for success the student failed to meet. When corrected, the student receives the feedback at the Self-level: I am a Failure (Hattie and Timperley, 2007). The corrected can only answer that they failed to reach their goals. Learners experiencing a collaborative approach think critically,

~~learning transferable concepts and practices.~~

The Focus of Feedback: Comprehensive or Narrow and Selective

Undeniably, there will be multiple areas for improvement. Sometimes, it is discouraging to look at everything a student has done incorrectly. A comprehensive, corrective stance can lead to an overwhelming amount of information the learner cannot fully address. On the other hand, a collaborative stance leads to a narrow and selective approach focused on what most matters in moving the student to the next learning progression phase, also known as the Zone of Proximal Development (Vygotsky, 1982).

A Corrective, Comprehensive Focus

It pains me to share this. I observed a corrective conference with Maria, a low-performing ESL student. Maria arrived at her first conference with a full page of handwritten text about the importance of technology. During the conference, one hundred eighty corrections for twenty-three topics were addressed. She returned to the revisions conference with three lines and the remainder of the page blank. The feedback was corrective and comprehensive, focusing on what Maria had written correctly and incorrectly, and in each instance.

Each correction was valid, as the composition was riddled with errors. Maria was reminded of lessons, resources, and procedures she should have applied. At this point, Maria could not write another word. While she wished to make a good grade and comply with her teacher's well-meaning advice, she couldn't. Yet, the question is: Was the feedback about Maria's compliance, or was it about a well-written essay? The answer is neither. The teacher wanted Maria to be a competent writer, and while I am reminded of the teacher's gentle approach, her feedback remains an extreme example of the detrimental impact of choosing a corrective, comprehensive stance.

Frankly, the more corrections students were asked to address, the fewer things they corrected. Furthermore, revisions resulted in little change to the overall quality of their writing, even if the required corrections were made. A corrective, comprehensive recitation of errors and what should have been done to correct them was not effective, hampering success and even causing regression. The Corrector answered the feedback questions *for* students: you are not reaching your goals. You are not making progress. You need to remember what you have been told to do.

Narrow and Selective Focus

In contrast, the collaborative stance maintains a narrow focus. The collaborator purposefully selects feedback, choosing to respond to the learner about the barrier most interfering with success (Elliot, et al., 2016; Ferris, 2014). In conferences where the collaborator's feedback focused on a single, deep feature affecting the reader's experience with the text, writers improved multiple features of their writing that were not even addressed in the conference—both deep (meaning) and surface (grammar and mechanics) features of sound writing.

The fewer things learners were asked to consider to better communicate their meaning, the more things they revised to develop all portions of the composition. Collaborators selected persistent, prevalent problems. Then, they discussed the solution and prompted the student to use those strategies and principles in other instances. Since many topics and instances were not the focus of the conference, the collaborator and learner were able to spend time on what to do about the problem, answering the final question never present with The Corrector: "Where to next?" and how to do so? (Hattie, 2009, p. 177).

Additionally, collaborators addressed deep features five to sixteen times more frequently than surface considerations. Conversely, the corrective stance referenced the surface features at a much higher ratio. But here's the boilerplate conclusion: students who received feedback through a focused, selective, and collaborative stance improved the quality of their compositions in multiple areas. Students who received feedback through a comprehensive and corrective stance were less successful in improving the quality of their work.

Application. As the collaborator with a narrow, selective focus, you follow four principles:

- Principle One: Focus on the main problem interfering with success.
- Principle Two: Focus on deep issues (critical attributes) in meaning and communication of understanding.
- Principle Three: Identify the main problem. Spend the rest of

~~the time focused on how to repair that problem.~~

- Principle Four: Allow the student to explain their response to you after applying the feedback. Feedback is a spiraling, formative cycle, not a closed summative loop (Costa and Kallick, 1995).

The explanation of the comprehensive versus a narrow approach to feedback was very specific to writing, and mentions of grammar and mechanics may make math teachers a little nauseous. Yet, there are some truths that make sense even to those who give feedback in other disciplines. Correctors focus on each and every mistake. However, reminding students of what they should have remembered and used did not result in improved performance. Corrective, comprehensive feedback is received as a summative judgement about their personal ability to learn: You have failed. In contrast, when empowered through an intensive focus on a single area posed as solutions for resolving the weakness into a strength, learners knew where they were in reaching their goals, the progress they were making, and how they could continue that process.

Questions, Directionality, and Dominance

Correctors and collaborators use questions differently. The distinctions change the directionality of conversation and set up important differences in dominance. Corrective feedback sequences establish the dominance of the teacher using behavioristic chaining that lead student thinking to a predetermined point. In contrast, collaborative feedback sequences use questions to reveal student thinking through a constructivist approach called funneling, inviting an exchange between teacher and learner.

Correction Sequences Dominate Student Thinking through Chaining

Corrective feedback sequences establish a pattern of questioning often called the Initiate, Respond, Evaluate (IRE) sequence (Durkin, 1978/1979). The Corrector asks a question; the student answers, usually not along the lines the teacher expected because students are trying to follow the *teacher's* line of thought. Essentially, students are guessing. The Corrector then evaluates the student's response for accuracy. The most poignant example of this was at the end of the conference with the dyslexic young man who struggled with word endings. We had moved into the goal-setting phase for the conference.

Teacher: Yeah. Elaborate. And we are going to work on the handwriting. (laughs)

Student: Yeah

Teacher: That's easy. We're also gonna use a what? What are you gonna use? We already talked about it.

Student: An eraser?

Teacher: (laughs) Yes, that potentially, too. But a dictionary and the thesaurus, remember? Yeah, because with the spelling, (S2S2 Coded Conference Transcript, p. 9-10).

The teacher had already moved from handwriting to a new concept, but the student didn't know that. While using a dictionary was not going to help him use the correct endings, the student incorrectly guessed what the teacher wanted him to say. His cognitive energy was not spent on learning the concepts but in unsuccessfully following the teacher's cognition.

This kind of questioning is called chaining. Chaining is a behavioristic technique developed by Skinner to break concepts into small bits, leading students to the right answers or thinking (1934). Unfortunately, most concepts are too complex to be broken down into small bits without also understanding how they fit into the whole concepts or processes of the discipline. Students do not need to be led to the right answers. Students must make their own neural connections for themselves (storage) so that they can use (retrieve) the ideas later (Atkinson and Shiffrin, 1968).

Chaining establishes the teacher as the dominant speaker and thinker. The Corrector gives extended responses or explanations of their thinking or understanding. In corrective conferences, students rarely responded with more than yes, no, or grunts. When students did give extended responses, they recited rules and expectations. In contrast, The Corrector talked two to six times more than the students. Chaining, leading questions, caused students to incorrectly answer the first two feedback questions: "Where am I going?" and "How

90

am I going?" "Where to next?" remained unanswered (Hattie, 2009, p.177).

Collaborative Conferences Promote Turn-Taking and Funneling

Collaborative conferences used funneling and clarification questions to narrow down where the learner's understanding broke down. Earlier, I shared an excerpt from a student struggling with writing a clear thesis statement. Look at the progression of questions the collaborator used to funnel down and identify where she needed to intervene:

What did you hear?

What do you mean by *clear*?

Do you know *why* it's not clear?

Ok. So that's where I jump in. The reason it's not clear to me as a reader…(Researcher's Journal, S1S1 Initial Conference, p 2-3).

The teacher did not seek a predetermined answer—she sought information *from* the student to know how to respond. The funneling approach invited active conversational exchanges between the collaborator and learners. Learners gave extended explanatory responses. While the collaborative teacher did give extended responses, comments were based on clarifying and responding to what the learner revealed. Ultimately, the conversation was more balanced: the collaborator spoke one to two times for every student utterance.

Application. As a collaborator, you follow three principles:

- Principle One: Ask open-ended, funneling questions to identify exactly where learner understanding breaks down.
- Principle Two: Invite back and forth exchanges to solicit ideas from learners.
- Principle Three: Offer extended responses as reactions to resolve issues in what learners reveal.

Regardless of the content, I have heard the following dictum: the person doing the talking is the person doing the learning. The Corrector talks more than students and asks questions for which they have a specific answer in mind. As a result, students spend their cognitive energy guessing what the teacher wants to know instead of internalizing needed concepts. In collaborative conferences, students are able to explain and communicate their understanding and struggles. These exchanges allow both the learner and collaborator to answer all three of Hattie's feedback questions (2009).

Feedback Types

Since we began with his three feedback questions, ending with Hattie's findings on the four types of feedback seems apropos. Hattie and Timperley (2007) identified four types of feedback: Task, Process, Self-Regulation, and Self. The Corrector and collaborative teachers use feedback types very differently.

Corrective Task and Process Types

The Corrector uses task feedback more often than any other type. Task feedback identifies what is right or wrong. Task level feedback can also check to see if the learner knows the correct answer or where to find missing information. In a corrective conference I viewed, the teacher had just identified a confusing thesis statement and was moving into the body of the composition.

> Teacher: I see the "to begin," so that's one body paragraph. What should I then see if you have another main idea?
>
> Student: Indention?
>
> Teacher: Right. Well, I need to see another body paragraph, don't I?
>
> Student: Oh yeah. [realizing] Mhmm.
>
> Teacher: I need to see another…[frames sections of the text] because you see that doesn't—I mean, let's try to keep our indentions kind of even, okay? I would say about a thumb's width. Okay? But I could tell this was the starting of a new paragraph [points to indention] But, do I see another paragraph… [starts scanning her finger down the margin] *ever?* (Researcher's Journal, S2S3, Charted Feedback, Excerpt 3).

In the excerpt above, The Corrector notes task feedback—what has been done correctly: the transition that begins the body paragraph and the indentation. The Corrector also gives task feedback about what has not been done correctly: the irregular indentions and the lack of another supporting body paragraph. The Corrector identifies what is correct and incorrect *for* the student.

The Corrector also used limited process feedback. Process level feedback can involve giving the rationale for why an answer is right or wrong and its impact on the meaning of other sections or concepts. Process level feedback can also offer specific and actionable strategies to resolve problems or ineffective processes. This level of feedback helps the learner know what to consider, change, or include with their thinking or in the task/product. In the excerpt above, the teacher does give a concrete strategy for keeping indentations consistent by using the thumb for spacing. Sometimes, The Corrector reads aloud from the text to help the writer experience reader struggles and meaning-making processes. Most of the Process strategies offered in corrective feedback asked the student to reread or use reference materials and handouts. Unfortunately, these requests were not often completed during corrections—and those that *were* accomplished failed to improve the overall quality of the writing.

Most frequently, Task and Process types of feedback answered only the first two feedback questions: "Where am I going?" and limited information about "How am I going?" (Hattie, 2009, p.177). Specific strategies to accomplish the corrections were limited, related to broken rules, and included little information about how to repair the problems.

Collaborative Feedback Sandwiches all Feedback Types

Collaborative conferences varied from corrective ones in how Task and Process feedback types were used. Task-level feedback was narrow, selective, and focused on student needs. Process level feedback offered concrete, actionable solutions as well as the rationale and impact of both error and correction. In addition, where Correctors did not, collaborators included Self-Regulatory and Self-feedback in conferences, sandwiching all feedback types for a cohesive unit of actionable data. Self-Regulatory feedback helps the learner monitor, evaluate, and reflect on their learning process or products. Self-feedback involves personal evaluations and observations. Hattie found that the praise elements in Self-feedback were detrimental to student learning because students did not have enough information to help the learner make changes (Hattie, 2009). In contrast, collaborative conferences involved distinct Self-feedback that was more attuned to learner intentions, characteristics, and background that helped the collaborator gain buy-in from the students or to make decisions about how the teacher would respond.

Let's take a peek at how the collaborator combined the four types of feedback in a conference with Spunky, a dyslexic male senior. Previously, the student refused to listen to the teacher's suggestions because he believed she was too liberal for his conservative sensitivities.

Self-Regulation	Teacher: So the first question I'm gonna ask you is: where do you think you're at with this right now?
Self-Regulation	Student: I feel like I'm done.
Self-Regulation	Teacher: Why do you feel like you're done?
Self-Regulation	Student: I don't see anything else to add to it.
Task, Self-Regulation, Self	Teacher: Okay. So if I could give you things to add to it, would you be open to that? I *don't* mean to tell you what to say. I promise not to fill you with a liberal agenda.
Self	Student: Well, this is the most liberal as I get so…
Self	Teacher: [laughs] It's actually more liberal than *I* get. Are you surprised? [Student gives her a wry look and then smiles]

Figure Two Researcher's Journal, S1S4 Charted Feedback, Excerpt 1.

The collaborator knew that she would have to respect Spunky's boundaries before he would accept any feedback. She opened with the self-regulatory probe to discern his awareness of his composition. Then, she needed to address his learner characteristics at the Self-level before he could accept what would come next. In addition, Process feedback worked differently in the collaborative conferences because the collaborator's strategy allowed the student to mention their own mistakes:

Teacher: [reading from text] Quote: teen pregnancy is strongly linked to poverty with the low-income level associated with higher teen birth rates. 52% of mothers on welfare had their first child in their teens. Low educational attainment among teen mothers affects their economic opportunities and earnings in later years. [takes a breath] Why money make it a viable reason...

Student: [while she is reading] I need to change that...

Teacher: Yeah. I know what you're saying; you just switched your words around. (Researcher's Journal, S1S4, Charted Feedback, Excerpt 2).

By hearing the text aloud as it was written, the student was able to identify errors he was unable to see when reading over the paper alone. Yet, he still wanted to argue about the introduction. It wasn't until the critical moment below when all four types of feedback came together that the halocline of Spunky's beliefs and standards of effective writing combined:

Task	Teacher: Okay. [almost gently] I *still* need you—as a reader— to introduce your point [taps the top of the paper] to me: the point of abortion in itself— whether it's controversial or not-
Process: strategy/ approach; Self: Agency	and you *don't* have to tell them which way you sway—and you *can leave* it neutral—
Task	but you *still* need to *introduce the idea.*
Process: Rationale	Because coming straight into the thesis is just a little jarring. It's just a little jarring because I don't know where to [pauses and picks up my phone]...Think of your essay like this physical phone. You know those little pop-ups on the back of the phones? I can't latch on to anything [trying to pick up the phone and lets her hands slide through/past]. Without an introduction, I can't hold on. So even though you may have told me all about the phone and how it works, because I don't have the pop-up, the phone's just going everywhere. I can't really latch on to it. I don't know where to anchor my thoughts to trace through the examples. [long pause]
Self - Regulation: evaluation	Does that make sense? (laughs at self) I'm just having a hard time— not with *what* you're saying -not with the *topic* you're writing about. I'm having a hard time getting in and buying into what you're saying because it [bounces with each of the next three words for emphasis] *starts so abruptly* that I don't even have time to [connect to] your reasons.

Figure Three: S1S4, Charted Feedback, Excerpt 9

Spunky agreed to add an introduction. The teacher and I were relieved. Yet: in this case—and almost every instance of effective revisions—the sandwiched feedback from multiple levels *directly correlated* with *changes* that *impacted the quality* of the writing. It was not until *all* levels were used that the student agreed to make a change. The collaborator understood who the learner was (Self), explained the success criteria (Task), and allowed the learner to make meaningful choices in the organizational strategy to introduce his thesis (Process). She followed with a rationale, explaining why an introduction was needed and the impact it had on the reader without it (Process). The feedback sequence ended with an explanation of how to know when an introduction was not effective by evaluating its abruptness (Self-Regulation).

Application. As Collaborator, you follow six principles:

- Principle One: Use Task feedback to identify a focused area that will improve the learning.
- Principle Two: Read and think aloud with the student's text or performance to give Process rationale of how their work impacts comprehension or gives evidence of understanding.
- Principle Three: Offer concrete, actionable strategies learners can use to correct their errors or thinking processes (Process).
- Principle Four: Use Self-Regulatory probes to determine where student learning breaks down and to offer ways to evaluate or monitor success and progress.
- Principle Five: Honor the learner's characteristics with Self-statements and considerations that leave them with dignity and agency to make their own decisions.
- Principle Six: Sandwich all four levels of feedback to trigger significant learning and response.

Let's connect this to what it means for people other than writing teachers: the Corrector primarily uses two types of feedback. Task feedback is used to tell what is right and wrong. Process rationale feedback is used to explain the rules the error violated, the importance of checking work, and the use of previous instruction. Basically, The Corrector uses feedback that tells the learner what they did wrong and what they forgot to use and remember. Students have general Process ideas about how to answer where to go next, but nothing specific to their needs and concrete actions to resolve the problems identified by The Corrector.

Students who collaborated in conferences where all four types of feedback were used made important revisions to improve their work (TASK), knew why they needed improvement to meet the success criteria (Process), employed concrete actions to make the change (Process), and utilized strategies to know if they had succeeded (Self-Regulation).

Triggering a Mechanical or Cognitive Response from Students

Ultimately, the student's response to feedback determines its effectiveness. Each stance is correlated with a reciprocal response from the student. In studying feedback to writing, I found that collaborative stances triggered a cognitive response from students up to three times more than teachers taking a corrective stance (Rose, 2021). When the teacher selects a corrective stance, the student's response is a simple-minded, mechanical approach that does not address the complexities of the writing process (Anson, 1989). The Corrector has already done the thinking. As a result, any changes are based on compliance unrelated to improving the quality of the paper or the reader's experience with the text.

Instead, when the teacher selects a collaborative stance, the learner's response activates cognitive processes that result in improved reader experiences and improvement in the overall quality of the composition. As I recoded all of the feedback from teachers in my dissertation studies, learners who received a higher ratio of cognitive vs. mechanical feedback improved the quality of their writing (Rose, 2021). Improved compositions received cognitive versus mechanical feedback at ratios between 1.18–2.82, while compositions that did not improve or declined in quality received cognitive versus mechanical feedback at ratios between 0.39–1.00 (Rose, 2021).

Learners respond to collaborative approaches and build awareness of where they are in terms of the success criteria and where they are on the continuum of improvement. Narrow and selective feedback supports and stretches the learner's Zone of Proximal Development. Collaborative stances invite active participation that allow learners to make important connections and decisions about how to apply feedback. And finally, collaborative stances utilized all four types of Hattie and Timperley's (2007) feedback to help learners identify what needed to change and why changes were necessary. In addition, the feedback sandwiches of all feedback types helped learners know exactly how to repair and evaluate the changes. Clearly, the learner's cognitive responses give insight into the critical attributes of effective feedback. As a professional learner, I can provide and seek feedback that meets those criteria and teach my learners to do the same.

References

Anson, C., (Ed.). (1989). *Writing and response: Theory, practice, and research.* National Council of Teachers of English.

Atkinson, R.C., and Shiffrin, R.M. (1968). Human memory: A proposed system and its control processes. In Spence, K.W. and Spence, J.T. (eds). *The Psychology of learning and Motivation 2, 89-195.* Academic Press.

Brookhart, S. M. (2004). Classroom assessment: tensions and intersections in theory and practice. *Teachers College Record, 106*(3), 429–458. https://doi.org/10.1111/j.1467-9620.2004.00346.x

Brookhart, S. M. (2007). Expanding views about formative classroom assessment: A review of the literature. In J. H. McMillan (Ed.), *Formative classroom assessment: Research, theory and practice* (pp. 43–62). Teachers College Press.

Carless, D. (2006). Differing perceptions in the feedback process. *Studies in Higher Education, 31*(2), 219–233. https://doi.org/10.1080/03075070600572132

Costa, A. L., & Kallick, B. (Eds.). (1995). *Assessment in the learning organization.* Association for Supervision and Curriculum Development.

Durkin, D. (1978/1979). What classroom observations reveal about reading comprehension instruction. *Reading Research Quarterly, (14),* 481-533. https://www.jstor.org/stable/747260

Dweck, C.S. (2007). *Mindset: The new psychology of success.* Ballantine Books.

Elliot, V., Baird, J., Hopfenbeck, AT.N., Ingram, J., Thompson, I., Usher, N., Zantout, M., Richardson, J., and Coleman, R. (2016). *A marked improvement? A review of the evidence on written marking.* University of Oxford, Education Endowment Foundation.

Ferris, D.K., (2014). Responding to student writing: Teachers' philosophies and practices. *Assessing Writing, 19,*(6-23). https://doi.org/10.1016/j.asw.2013.09.004

Fisher, D., Frey, N., and Hattie, J. (2018). *Assessment capable learners.* Corwin.

Hattie, J. C. (2009). *Visible learning: A synthesis of over 800 meta-analyses relating to achievement.* Routledge. https://doi.org/10.4324/9780203887332

Hattie, J. C., Gan, M., and Brooks, C. (2017). Instruction based on feedback. In *Handbook of research on learning and instruction* (pp. 290-324). Taylor and Francis.https://doi.org/10.4324/9780203839089

Hattie, J., & Timperley, H. (2007). The power of feedback. *Review of Educational Research, 77*(1), 81–112. https://doi.org/10.3102/003465430298487

Kluger, A.N., and DeNisi, A. (1996). The effects of feedback interventions on performance: A historical review, a meta-analysis, and a preliminary feedback intervention theory. *American Psychological Association, Inc. 119*(2), 254-284 https://doi.org/10.1037/0033-2909.119.2.254

Mory, E. H. (2004). Feedback research review. In D. Jonassen (Ed), *Handbook of research on educational communications and technology* (pp. 745–783). Lawrence Erlbaum Associates.

Narciss, S. (2008). Feedback strategies for interactive learning tasks. In J. M. Spector, M. D. Merrill, J. Van Merrienboer, & M. P. Driscoll (Eds.), *Handbook of research on educational communications and technology* (3rd ed., pp. 125–143). Erlbaum. https://doi.org/10.1007/978-1-4614-3185-5

Rose, S. (2021). *Feedback in the writing conference.* [Unpublished doctoral dissertation]. Texas Tech University.

Rosenblatt, L. (1978). *The reader, the text, the poem: The transactional theory of the literary work.* Southern Illinois Press.

Sadler, D. R. (2010). Beyond feedback: Developing student capability in complex appraisal. *Assessment & Evaluation in Higher Education, 35*(5), 535–550. https://doi.org/10.1080/02602930903541015

Skinner, B. F. (1934). The extinction of chained reflexes. *Proceedings of the National Academy of Sciences of the United States of America, 20*(4), 24–7. https://doi.org/10.1073/pnas.20.4.234

Vygotsky, L. (1986). Thought and language (A. Kozulin, Ed). Massachusetts Institute of Technology Press. https://doi.org/10.1017/s0272263100008172

William. D. (2011). *Embedded formative assessment.* Solution Tree.

Chapter 7

Critical Literacy Instruction in Uncertain Times

Elizabeth Davis Jones

Abstract

In the midst of political, medical, and social tensions, educators find themselves navigating difficult spaces. Interrupted learning has magnified existing educational inequities, unpredictable learning challenges, and students' disenfranchisement with literacy. Educators have embraced professional learning despite these struggles to better prepare themselves for uncertainty. In this chapter, I will introduce cosmopolitan critical literacy as a noteworthy theory to reconceptualize literacy instruction and examine how a broadened sense of humanity and critical literacy provides diverse opportunities for nurturing global citizenship. The chapter will closely examine the implications of cosmopolitan critical literacy on digital literacy, citizenship, creativity, and professional learning.

Introduction

After months of interrupted formal education, students now sit in our classrooms awaiting instruction. More than 1.6 billion students globally experienced an abrupt disruption to learning due to the school closures related to COVID-19 (Murali, 2021). For some, they have not been in a formal school setting since March 2020. The state of unfinished learning amplifies the existing educational inequities and learning achievement gaps. Returning to in-person instruction is not business as usual. The world has changed, and so have our students. Educators must find a way to meet their students' social–emotional, and learning needs amidst complex literacy demands.

Many parents, school districts, and legislators believe students need more literacy support caused by unfinished learning (Betebenner & Wenning, 2021; Dorn et al., 2021). A recent analysis comparing Fall 2020 and Fall 2021 reading performance found that more upper elementary and middle school students, especially those in vulnerable communities, are in need of reading intervention (Curriculum Associates, 2021). With such a large population of students needing differentiated literacy instruction and the pressure of mandated end-of-the-year test assessments, the temptation to focus on re-teaching foundational literacy such as phonics, word recognition, and fluency, is appealing (Mesmer, 2020). Today's students need more than foundational literacy skills. They need authentic and engaging ways to practice the skills (Alvermann, 2008; Bean & Dunkerly, 2012; Buchholz et al., 2020; Taffe & Bauer, 2013). This means that teachers need to find instructional practices through pedagogical studies, professional learning communities, and self-reflection. What has always worked in the past will likely not work the same way, if at all, in the current academic environment. As technology and literacy have changed, teachers must change instruction to match.

Focusing on just foundational literacy skills is not enough; a skills-based approach to instruction will only continue to disenfranchise students from literacy rather than building their literacy capacity (Gonzalez et al., 2018). The advancement of technology and social practices have expanded the definition of literacy. Reading, writing, and communicating are no longer paperbound. Texts now include both paper and multimodal text (Kress, 2000; Leu et al., 2014; Cope & Kalantzis, 2000). As a rapidly changing force, digital media permeates the classroom, creating many questions, complexities, and potential for literacy instruction to prepare students to be active, literate citizens who enjoy lifelong learning. While multimodal texts offer great potential in the classroom, the ubiquitous influence of multimodal texts on students' literacy practices creates challenges for traditional literacy instruction (Harper et al., 2010; Leu et al., 2014; Gee, 2017). A changing world calls for a remix in literacy pedagogy and instructional practices. Educators have a rare opportunity to transform their classroom by merging previous professional learning on critical literacy pedagogy and everyday technology practices within the context of their classroom.

Cosmopolitan Critical Literacy

Cosmopolitan critical literacy is a theoretical framework that broadens the current definition of critical literacy to encompass critical global issues of human rights and provides a framework for educators to change their classroom with theory into practice. (Bean, 2016) Literacy is more than a cognitive function. "Literacy involves communicating, evaluating, synthesizing, and connecting to social practices" (Gee, 2003, p. 17). Before the pandemic, researchers, educators, and corporations called for critical literacy instruction in the classroom. Critical literacy promotes reading comprehension (Fisher, 2008) and problem-solving skills and prepares our students with essential global competencies (CCSSO & Asia Society, 2011). With our world becoming a global digital society due to quarantines and lockdowns, a more global perspective in our classroom literacy practices is needed (Buchholz et al., 2020). Now is the time for teachers to offer students literacy experiences to develop the global and technological competencies with cosmopolitan critical literacy.

What is Cosmopolitan Critical Literacy?

Our world's current political, economic, and educational tensions call for cosmopolitan critical literacy. Cosmopolitan critical literacy supports instructional practices that encourage civic engagement by accepting social differences with opportunities to use digital media to address global human rights and social justice (Bean et al., 2016; Bean & Dunkerly, 2015; Dunkerly-Bean, 2013, Dunkerly-Bean et al., 2014). The deconstruction of media messages and the creation and sharing of digital media serve as authentic literacy experiences that promote active learning while simultaneously developing "an informed critical citizenry" (Bean, 2016, p. 17). Cosmopolitan critical literacy is grounded in human rights education (Dunkerly-Bean; 2013; Bean & Dunkerly-Bean, 2016). Students practice deconstructing text and digital media through questioning, discussion, and reflection (Kellner & Share, 2007). Therefore, cosmopolitan critical literacy provides a framework for educators to update their current literacy pedagogy and instructional practices to nurture students' understanding of others through evaluation, deconstruction, and problem-solving of power and silence issues in relation to local and global human rights (Bean,

2016; Dunkerly-Bean, 2013; Dunkerly-Bean & Bean, 2015).

Potential for Reconceptualizing Instruction and Classroom Practices

The primary concern of cosmopolitan critical literacy is to transform educational and social inequities (Dunkerly-Bean, 2013). Cosmopolitan critical literacy in the classroom offers teachers a way to navigate difficult spaces, capitalizing on previous literacy professional learning. Through the use of Professional Learning Communities (PLC) and self-reflection, the learning gap and disenfranchisement can be bridged as teachers discover the ability to effectively incorporate cosmopolitan critical literacy into classrooms. Because cosmopolitan critical literacy is designed to nurture the acceptance of difference in others using digital media, it can help to reconceptualize instruction and classroom practices. When teachers take the time to reflect on the practices they currently use, what they have learned, and discuss those practices with their colleagues, it opens the door for communication among their professional community to consider necessary instructional changes to meet the individual needs of students in the learning environment, especially those who are disenfranchised with literacy. Using cosmopolitan critical literacy provides an opportunity to reconceptualize traditional academic literacy instruction by developing students' global citizenship, digital literacy skills, and creativity and innovation.

Global Citizenship

Our world has become virtually connected through online spaces. This transnational connection affords students to explore their acceptance of other's differences and their responsibilities as global citizens. Educators can integrate everyday practices students use with academic literacy instruction to assist students in accepting others to generate solutions to local and global issues while designing multimodal texts. Just as professional learning provides teachers opportunities to collaborate and learn together, students need opportunities to collaborate and reflect with their teachers. This collaborative learning environment not only builds teacher-student rapport but also provides educators and students to cultivate a student-focused professional learning community, where teachers and students learn and reflect from and with each other (Gates, 2018). Using cosmopolitan critical literacy as the framework establishes a safe environment based on this learning community's human rights and social justice. This safe environment enables students to experience the concept of democracy and encourages a deeper appreciation for responsibilities and global competencies to become active, global citizens (Buhholz et al., 2020).

Being a global citizen means seeing oneself as a part of the global community. Regardless of age, students become information literate citizens; students are empowered and develop empathy for others. As students develop compassion and empathy for others, critical literacy becomes a part of being human (Gee, 2017). As more United States classrooms become increasingly composed of transnational, multilingual students, literacy instruction needs to support all learners. Cosmopolitan critical literacy instruction capitalizes upon the knowledge brought to the classroom (Rodriquez, 2013), experiences, and cultures of students to help students navigate social contexts and advocate for others and global issues using digital media (Dunkerly-Bean, 2014; Bean & Dunkerly-Bean, 2015). Equity and inclusion become a product of cosmopolitan critical literacy.

Using current events and books with themes of global concerns, teachers can facilitate critical discussions. Students' interests in local and global issues offer multiple opportunities for cosmopolitan critical literacy discussions using global youth literature. Global youth literature is children and young adult books written from an authentic intercultural and global perspective. Integrating global youth literature in the classroom provides new opportunities for critical discussions exploring the sociopolitical underpinnings of our world. Global youth literature highlights the interdependence of people from around the world. These books celebrate our world diversity and offer new perspectives on life and living in other places outside of one's Nation. Global youth literature introduces students to new sociocultural contexts of power and language. By reading global youth literature and having critical discussions, educators can challenge students' habitual ways of being and create new ways of thinking and being (Kim, 2021). Lists and reviews of children and young adult books for a global youth literature initiative in the classroom are available at https://wowlit.org/.

Questions grounded in cosmopolitan critical literacy help interweave human rights and social justice in relation to global citizenship naturally through literacy instruction, and it helps facilitate authentic student discussion. Dunkerly-Bean and Bean (2015) offered five critical questions to help students consider issues in global youth literature by creating a questioning stance as they read and respond to texts (p. 3).

1. Who benefits from the way gender, race, and culture are portrayed?
2. What identities (global and local) are possible in this text?
3. How does this text position self to Others?
4. How would this text change if it was situated within a different context or culture?
5. What is my responsibility to Others in this text?

These reflective questions encourage students to explore the power of language and how they, as students, might take appropriate action to facilitate change. By combining global youth literature with cosmopolitan critical literacy, global cultures' historical and sociocultural circumstances are represented in the classroom (Botehelo & Sorrow, 2016). For multilingual learners and students disenfranchised from traditional literacy instruction, these unique learning experiences provide new invitations to learn with and from one another. Students can use the language of the text to build vocabulary and to establish a new understanding of diversity and power (Luke, 2012), boosting both reading and writing skills. Students learn to analyze and evaluate texts and develop a sense of their responsibility to others. The graphic novel, *The Breadwinner*, by Deborah Ellis (2017), set in Kabul, Afghanistan, is an example of global youth literature available for classroom use. For students who ask, "Why do I need to learn about someone else's life?" Ellis's book offers an avenue to answer their question. As students read, they are confronted with new experiences many protagonists in classic children's and young adult literature have not had. Reading this book welcomes students who have emigrated from Afghanistan not only to see themselves in literature but also give them opportunities to vet the reality of the events in the book. Students who may feel invisible in the classroom now serve as primary sources. Transnational students provide a valuable perspective for students who have not had the same experiences (Botelho & Sowell, 2016). Yet, students and educators can discover commonalities that promote acceptance of differences through sharing.

A critical pedagogy that values students' funds of knowledge improves academic literacy and disrupts inequities in our classrooms (Moll, 2019). Within these settings, teachers acknowledge literacy instruction grounded in cosmopolitan critical literacy facilitates a deeper understanding of content and encourages advocacy towards changing current social, cultural, and political issues (Vasquez et al., 2013). As our world becomes more globally connected, cosmopolitan critical literacy assists in connecting others through commonalities rather than differences. Not only do teachers and students become aware of human rights, but they can also critically analyze media messages in relation to their sociocultural context and audience positions to consider ways to create equitable circumstances for others, not only locally, but globally (Luke, 2012; Dunkerly-Bean, 2013).

Digital Literacy

Digital communications have the potential of introducing students to new perspectives in relation to experiences, concerns, and issues of human rights and social justice as the world are digitally connected (Bean & Moni, 2003; Buckingham, 2005; Dunkerly, 2013; Bean & Dunkerly, 2016). Media is more than news broadcasting. Media, the plural form for medium, are forms of communicating ideas, including paper and digital texts with images and sound bites. A barrage of digital media surrounds students daily. Students interact with technology daily and must be skilled in navigating, understanding, and making meaning from deictic, constantly changing texts (Cioro et al., 2008; Cope & Katalntzis, 2000). Being an information literate citizen and reflecting upon messages in media demands active conceptual knowledge and critical evaluation of dynamic, multimodal texts (Buckingham, 2005; Coiro et al., 2008). Screen time has increased dramatically for students. Children from 18 months to 17 years of age consume media (CommonSense, n.d.). A constant consumption of dynamic information does not ensure students are critically thinking about media texts and messages, despite being digital natives (Pensky, 2001). For students to understand embedded messages of media, critical digital literacy skills are essential. Critical digital literacy supports academic literacy and helps students deconstruct fake news, misinformation, and propaganda in relation to local and global concerns (Sales, 2016). "Children develop media literacy even in the absence of explicit attempts to encourage and promote it" (Buckingham, 2005). Therefore, aiding students in developing critical media literacy is essential for academic literacy in the K-12 curriculum. Using cosmopolitan critical literacy to guide instruction will allow students to develop critical digital literacy skills (Kellner & Share, 2007b).

One way to develop students' critical digital literacy skills is to provide instruction on creating and sharing digital media. By constructing a representation of their ideas using various digital tools, critical digital literacy skills and strategies are developed. Not only are the students developing vital literacy skills that increase vocabulary development, comprehension, and writing, but teachers' literacy pedagogy shifts to a critical stance. Students must consider their stance, writing technique, and ways of illustrating their complex ideas in meaningful ways. To understand what they have read, students need to think deeply about their thoughts and consider the most effective way to share their thinking with others. Composing digital media becomes a socially situated literacy practice in online environments to experiment with expressing personal narratives, viewpoints, and opinions using a variety of media (Buchhholz et al., 2020). Using a combination of cosmopolitan critical literacy and critical digital literacy skills, students develop their understanding of digital literacy as well as the necessary skills to respectfully respond to those with differing opinions with civic engagement. In addition, students come to understand their rights and responsibilities of appropriate digital media usage as they consider the audience and tone of their intended messages.

Cosmopolitan critical literacy's unique design of exploring human rights in relation to global issues provides an authentic audience for student interaction that offers meaningful literacy experiences. For elementary and secondary students, especially those who are disenfranchised from traditional academic literacy instruction, digital activities and meaningful literacy experiences can simultaneously develop critical literacy and understanding of others and the world as classroom activities mimic the same social practices available outside of school. Some educational applications that support these global interactions are www.epals.com (ePals), https://info.flipgrid.com, (Flipgrid), and https://edublogs.org (Edublogs). All three apps are available to offer a pathway for students to connect, collaborate, and share digital media with students from different countries in the world.

Authentic Literacy Experiences

Email, blogging, and vlogging are outside-of-school social practices many students follow. ePals is a platform that allows educators to connect with other educators and their students to communicate with other classrooms based on age, subject, language, and location. Teachers make the initial contact, and then between the teachers, communication about literacy is facilitated through email. Flipgrid also provides international collaborations for students as students can create, edit, and share digital media creations using videos, emojis, and multiple filters within the app. Within the Flipgrid app, GridPals are international classrooms for international conversation. Instead of using Flipgrid for video responses to teachers and classmates, GridPals offers an authentic global audience in a safe environment to learn from other students and discuss relevant issues and concerns.

Edublogs is a platform designed specifically for student blogging. Teachers can create classroom blogs, or students can create their own blogs to share with others using the platform. Blogs can be hidden from search engines' indexes and can be filtered and monitored by the teacher. Teachers are encouraged to make sure these applications meet district requirements for the collection of student data. All discussion is monitored and filtered, making it safe and appropriate. If teachers plan on using any of these apps with students under 13 years of age, they must be sure to make sure to obtain parent permission and set aside time to approve posts so the conversations keep flowing.

All three of these apps allow teachers and students a safe environment to develop reading, writing, voice, and design skills through authentic practice with a choice of media. Because of the way these apps are designed, students learn to create, use, and interpret media critically, they have opportunities to use cosmopolitan critical literacy to analyze media in relation to audience and power; thus, empowering students to produce alternative media texts that challenge dominant social messages and stereotypes while still being respectful to those with differing ideas and opinions (Kellner & Share, 2007a). These platforms also provide much flexibility in the classroom. Most classwork, as a result of literacy instruction, can also be exchanged. As students finish independent reading books, they have a choice of media to create book talks and reviews. These creations can be shared with their virtual classmates on the apps. In return, they receive digital responses to their thinking from meaningful discussions surrounding topics vital to them. These apps also support project-based inquiry and culminating projects to literacy units. For instance, students can research an important global topic close to their hearts, such as immigration. The students then work in groups to research attitudes and stereotypes surrounding immigration experiences and human rights. As a culminating activity or summative assessment, students might consider producing a video to show their understanding and reflections (YouTube, 2014).

Videos and other digital media such as this also serve as critical community discussions for transnational students and parents about immigration. The video assists students in having a voice in a global concern. Students learn that events in different parts of the world impact their community, democracy, and nation. Cosmopolitan critical literacy becomes innate as they reflect and design their own text in response to the text they have deconstructed. The digital media would become the mentor texts for the classroom, shifting the literacy pedagogy from foundation literacy skills to a critical literacy lens. This also serves as professional learning opportunities for teachers to plan and discuss instructional practices through cosmopolitan critical literacy and digital literacy with other teachers. In a way, students would be creating their professional learning communities in order to understand the world around them. By accepting others' differences, students can find common ground with their peers, whether locally or globally, and begin working together to understand social and cultural issues while making connections with critical literacy in the academic world.

Creativity and Innovation

Incorporating digital media into the classroom also provides students opportunities to foster new creative and innovative skills. "When people find their medium, they discover their real creative strengths and come into their own" (Robinson, 2011, p. 139). When students have opportunities to explore multimodal texts, they are afforded the freedom to imagine. The created multimodal texts offer multiple vantage points of the voice being heard, understood, and validated (Robinson, 2011). When ideas are produced using one's imagination, students are empowered to design their ideas in various ways and are also empowered to consider their futures (Robinson, 2011).

Developing multimodal texts nurtures the necessary visual, linguistic, and analytic skills necessary to be creative, problem-solve, and consider new options. Students can creatively experiment with digital media tools when responding to literature and writing. They can create unique digital media, which leads to innovations for using popular apps. Snapchat and TikTok both provide an opportunity to teach students to share their learning. While many school districts, educators, and parents do not support Snapchat and TikTok in the classroom, the literacy practices developed through utilizing these apps can provide the benefits of cosmopolitan critical literacy and professional learning opportunities. Tara M. Martin (2017), in her blog provides a creative and safe way of integrating Snapchat literacy skills into the classroom with BookSnaps. BookSnaps (Martin, 2017) are exciting ways to breathe new life into reader responses or writing prompts. Using district approved software, such as Google Slides, Microsoft Office 365, or even an app called Book Creator, students can capture and document evidence of their reading, thinking, and critical analysis and use this evidence to create a digital response which can then be posted on Snapchat and TikTok accounts. By posting their BookSnaps (Martin, 2017), students participate in critical online discussions and problem-solving related to literacy and global issues. Students are being creative in designing new media and are also practicing and polishing their foundational and critical literacy skills. BookSnaps also provide educators with new professional learning and an innovative way to reimagine literacy instruction in the classroom. The BookSnaps can be shared on a school Snapchat, TikTok, or Twitter account.

#BookTok is also another avenue to engage students in digital media creation and literacy. #BookTok is a community on TikTok that reviews and recommends books. The community has been recognized for inspiring a return to reading books and has even helped launch new authors (Murray, 2021). Making BookToks invites students to join the community and the conversation. Students can create their own BookToks by combining sounds, video, and pictures. There is no need to have students' pictures or voices added. #BookToks could serve as another literacy professional learning opportunity. #Book-Toks videos can be downloaded and shared in the classroom and on the app to encourage analysis and evaluation. Creating, discussing, and posting #BookToks are social literacy practices that can include cosmopolitan critical literacy in understanding the difference in preferences of literature choice and digital literacy with the choice of media used to promote that literature. Largely because of the media that already exists in student lives through these apps, literacy practices now become relevant to students where it was miniscule or absent before. Teachers can always post anonymously for students (with permission) on a class TikTok enabling many voices to be heard and modeling an innovative use of social media to make change.

Implications for Professional Learners

Instruction in the classroom is no longer about finding the main idea or about reading environmental print but sharing ideas so others can hear individual voices. This creative literacy experience also invites students to be innovative with their learning as they discover new ways to share using social media and educational apps. Students who do not have access to these platforms are still able to have their voices heard, and the classroom instruction becomes more equitable, engaging, and accepting while learning about others.

Educator Literacy Knowledge and Capacity

The difficult times in the classroom are a call for educators to capitalize on previously learned literacy to implement knowledge in a new way in the classroom. Cosmopolitan critical literacy provides a framework to encourage global citizenship, digital literacy, and creative innovation while supporting foundational and critical literacy skills necessary for student success. The virtual instructional skills educators developed when COVID-19 caused the disruption of face-to-face instruction are still applicable. Literacy impacts all aspects of a students' life. Connecting academic instruction with social practices can refresh literacy instruction and help students overcome their disenfranchisement. Face-to-face instruction framed by cosmopolitan critical literacy is a flexible infrastructure of literacy instruction which contributes to developing informational literacy as students prepare to participate as global citizens based upon the professional learning, reflection, and the context of the classroom.

Professional development is a structured professional learning that results in refinement of educator knowledge, practices and improvement in student academic growth" (Darling-Hammond et al., 2017). Therefore, PLC is better situated to meet teachers' evolving professional learning needs, literacy coaches, instructional coaches, and administrators (Darling-Hammond et al., 2017; Bates & Morgan, 2018). Using Cosmopolitan critical literacy contributes to teachers' literacy capacity and shapes a new pathway to critical literacy using digital media. Through the use of PLC, teachers can learn how to provide students with opportunities to design digital media that display their learning and thinking and build essential communication skills reflective of both online discussions and face-to-face interactions. Blogging, vlogging, and communicating with various media tools yield meaningful classroom activities for students to connect, comprehend, analyze, evaluate, and design complex dynamic fiction, non-fiction, and digital texts (Coiro et al., 2008; Cope & Kalantzis, 2000; Tanti, 2012).

Critical Literacy Instruction

Cosmopolitan critical literacy affords educators the opportunity to develop the "sophisticated forms of teaching" (Darling-Hammond et al., 2017, p. 1) practices required for students currently in the classrooms. Global citizenship, critical digital literacy, and creativity and innovation are ways cosmopolitan critical literacy can transform one's classroom. Apps offer meaningful literacy experiences for communication, such as email, blogging, and vlogging. When these activities are combined with global literature and creative innovation, engagement can improve, helping students who are disenfranchised with school find a new interest. Cosmopolitan critical literacy can also inspire education through empowerment. Being able to implement effective change from professional learning enables teachers to make changes necessary for the context of their classroom based upon the strengths, needs, and interests of their students. Success and learning are contagious, especially when students are the focal point for change. Education reform depends upon the individual teacher's literacy capacity

(Stoll et al., 2006). In addition, instructional improvements in literacy instruction also rely upon the contextual changes each teacher makes in their classroom based upon the dynamics and needs of their students (Barnett & Fallon, 2007). Therefore, cosmopolitan critical literacy will not look the same in any two classrooms. Dunkerly-Bean et al. (2014) call for more contextual examples and models as cosmopolitan critical literacy is still young in the field of literacy. Professional learners can no longer count on external professional developments to meet the dynamic nature of literacy instruction (Barnett, J. & Fallon, 2007).

Professional Learning Communities

Discussions in PLC are powerful. The time has come for professional learning communities (PLC) to begin the essential conversations of using cosmopolitan critical literacies in the classroom. With COVID-19 and other catastrophic global issues dominating the headlines, no one, not even students, are left unaffected. The PLC offers a safe environment for educators to reflect upon new navigational tools to refine their pedagogy and instructional skills by examining theory and its connection to instructional practices. Frequent discussions enable educators to clarify their own critical questions and inspire professional learners to achieve the much needed literacy instruction transformation in their classroom (Sims & Fletcher-Wood, 2020).

Investigation of cosmopolitan critical literacy in PLC provides professional learners new perspectives for critical literacy pedagogy and instruction and opportunities to experience critical literacy in action (Stoll et al., 2006). New perspectives and experiences equip educators with new skill sets and afford teachers and students opportunities to learn with one another within a difficult space. With cosmopolitan critical literacy as a framework for literacy instruction, the learning space difficulties can become fewer as students engage in much-needed difficult conversations about global issues rather than difficulty in learning foundational literacy skills. Having students discuss and design as the focus rather than ability and strategy enables the learning environment to become more foundational in student-centered learning, supportive of critical literacy development and acceptance of others.

Conclusion

Extending critical literacy instruction in the classroom can no longer be ignored. With the purpose of literacy education being to develop information-literate individuals who are active citizens in a creative and ethical society, diverse students who are maturing readers, writers, designers, and global citizens, cannot simply read books and learn strategies as they sit in classrooms awaiting engaging instruction that is relevant to them (Livingstone & Helsper, 2010). Cosmopolitan critical literacy practices hold the potential to build identities of agentic, global citizens *while* developing literacy skills and meeting academic outcomes. Cosmopolitan critical literacy provides educators the skills to transform literacy instruction from skill-based and test-centric practices to a critical literacy pedagogy while embracing human rights and social justice. Using digital media, reading, writing, and communicating about global youth literature nurtures students' sociocultural stances and provides moments to examine their responsibility to others as active global citizens.

Much professional learning from the past has provided educators with many critical literacy, collaborative, and educational apps to use as transformative tools. To overcome the struggles in the classroom, teachers can use past professional learning techniques and cosmopolitan critical literacy to reframe academic literacy instruction. If school districts do not approve apps, there must be advocates for these essential authentic experiences. Educators have the power to change their classrooms and still meet mandated outcomes and state assessments. Teacher agency influences students' hopes and voices. By helping students develop a reflective and critical stance, educators are not only creating opportunities for students to develop agency. Still, they are also offering authentic situations to apply literacy as global citizens. This chapter should serve as a resource for beginning a much-needed conversation. Cosmopolitan critical literacy, in turn, will provide an empowering critical stance for teachers and students to navigate uncertain times.

References

Alvermann, D. E. (2008). Why bother theorizing adolescent online literacies for classroom practice and research. *Journal of Adolescent & Adult Literacy, 52*(1), 9-20. hppt://doi:10.1598/JAAL.52.1.2

Barnett, J. & Fallon, G. (2007). Understanding a teacher's knowledge: Understanding a teacher's knowledge of classroom community. *McGill Journal of Education, 42*(1), 120-141.

Bates, C.C. & Morgan, D.N. (2018). Seven Elements of Effective Professional Development. *The Reading*

Teacher, 71(5), 623-626. https://doi.org/10.1002/trtr.1674

Bean, T. W. (2016). Digital media and cosmopolitan critical literacy: Research and practice. In B. Guzzetti & M. Lesley (Eds.), *The social impact of digital media* (pp. 46-66). Hershey, PA: Information Science Reference. http://doi: 10.4018/978-1-4666-8310-5.ch003

Bean, T.W. & Dunkerly, J. (2012). Adolescent literacy: Looking back and moving forward in the global flow. *Journal of Adolescent & Adult Literacy 55*(8), 669-670.

Bean, T. W. & Dunkerly-Bean, J. M. (2015). Expanding conceptions of adolescent literacy research and practice: Cosmopolitan theory in educational contexts. *Australian Journal of Language and Literacy 38*(1), 46-54.

Bean, T.W. & Dunkerly, J. (2016). At the intersection of creativity and civic engagement: Adolescents' literacies in action. *Journal of Adolescent & Adult Literacy 60*(3), 247-253.

Bean, T.W. & Moni, K.B. (2003). Developing students' critical literacy: Exploring identity construction in young adult fiction. Journal of Adolescent & Adult Literacy 46(8), 638-648.

Betebenner, D.W. & Wenning, R.J. (2021, January). *Understanding pandemic learning loss and learning recovery: The role of student growth and statewide testing.* National Center for Improvement of Educational Assessment. https://www.nciea.org/articles/understanding-pandemic-learning-loss-and-learning-recovery-role-student-growth-statewide.

Botelho, M.J. & Sowell, N. (2016, August 6). *Teaching global children's literature: What to read and how to read.* Retrieved December 18, 2021, from https://www.edweek.org/leadership/opinion-teaching-global-childrens-literature-what-to-read-and-how-to-read/2016/08

Buchholz, B.A., DeHart, J., & Moorman, G. (2020). Digital citizenship during a global pandemic: Moving beyond digital literacy. *Journal of Adolescent & Adult Literacy 64*(1),11-17. https://doi.org/10.1002/jaal.1076

Buckingham, D. (2005). The media literacy of children and young people: A review of the research literature. Retrieved from https://discovery.ucl.ac.uk/id/eprint/10000145.

Coiro, J., Knobel, M., Lankshear, C., & Leu, D. (2008). Central issues in new literacies and new literacies research. In J. Coiro, M. Knobel, C. Lankshear & D. Leu (eds.), *Handbook of Research on New Literacies.* (pp. 1-21). Lawrence Erlbaum Associates, Taylor and Francis Group.

Cope, W. & Kalantzis, M. (2000). *Multiliteracies: Literacy learning and the design of social futures.* Routledge.

Curriculum Associates (2021). *Understanding student learning; Insights from fall 2021.* https://www.curriculumassociates.com/research-and-efficacy/unfinished-learning-research

Common Sense Media. (n.d.). *How much screen time is OK for my kid(s)?* Cellphone parenting: exploring questions by age. Retrieved December 18, 2021, from https://www.commonsensemedia.org/screen-time/how-much-screen-time-is-ok-for-my-kids

CCSSO & Asia Society. (2011) Global Competence Framework. *California Global Education Project.* http://calglobaled.org/global-competence

Dunkerly-Bean, J. (2013). Reading the world: The possibilities for literacy instruction framed within human rights education. *Language and Literacy, 15*(2), 40-55. doi:10.20360/G2T019

Dunkerly-Bean, J. & Bean, T.W. (2015). Exploring human rights and cosmopolitan critical literacy with global young adult literature multimodal text sets. *The New England Reading Association Journal, 50*(2), 1-8.

Dunkerly-Bean, J., Bean, T.W., & Alnajjar, K. (2014). Seeking Asylum: Adolescents explore the crossroads of human rights education and cosmopolitan critical literacy. Journal of Adolescent & Adult Literacy, 58(3), 230-241. https://doi.org/10.1002/jaal.349

Darling-Hammond, L., Hyler, M. E., Gardner, M. (2017). *Effective Teacher Professional Development.* Learning Policy Institute. https://learningpolicyinstitute.org/product/effective-teacher-professional-development-report

Dorn, E., Hancock, B, Sarakatsannis, J., & Viruleg, E. (2020). *Covid-19 and learning loss-disparities grow and students need help.* https://www.mckinsey.com/industries/public-and-social-sector/our-insights/covid-19-and-learning-loss-disparities-grow-and-students-need-help

Ellis, D. (2017). *The breadwinner: A graphic novel.* Groundwood Books/House of Anansi Press.

Fisher, A. (2008). Teaching comprehension and critical literacy: investigating guided reading in three primary classrooms. *Literacy, 42*(1), 19-28. ***https://doi.org/10.1111/j.1467-9345.2008.00477.x***

Gates, S. (2018, October 18). *Benefits of collaboration.* NEA. Retrieved December 19, 2021, from https://www.nea.org/professional-excellence/student-engagement/tools-tips/benefits-collaboration

Gee, J.P. (2000). Teenagers in new times: a new literacy studies perspective. *Journal of Adolescent and Adult literacy, 43*(5), 412-420.

Gee, J.P. (2017). *Teaching, learning, literacy in our high-risk high-tech world: a framework for becoming human.* Teachers College Press.

Gonzales, N., MacIntyre, S., & Beccar-Varela, P. (2018, February 22). Leveled literacy intervention for secondary students: results from a randomized controlled trial in Oakland schools. *Mathematica Policy Research Reports*. Princeton.

Harper, H., Bean, T.W., & Dunkerly, J. (2010). Cosmopolitanism, globalization, and the field of adolescent literacy. *Canadian and International Education, 39*(3), 1. https://doi.org/10.5206/cie-eci.v39i3.9159

Kellner, D. & Share, J. (2007a). *Critical media literacy, democracy, and the reconstruction of education*. In D. Macedo & S.R. Steinberg (Eds.), *Media literacy: A reader* (pp. 3-23). Peter Lang Publishing.

Kellner, D. & Share, J. (2007b). Critical media literacy is not an option. *Learning Inquiry, 1*(1), 59-69. https://doi:10.1007/s11519-007-0004-2.

Kim, HeeYoung (2021, December 1). *How to Read Global Children's Literature*.National Council of Teachers of English. Retrieved on December 18, 2021, from https://ncte.org/blog/2021/12/read-global-childrens-literature

Kress, G (2000). Multimodality: Challenges to thinking about language. *TESOL Quarterly, 34*(2), 337-340. https://doi-org.lib-e2.lib.ttu.edu/10.2307/3587959

Leu, D. J., Kizner, C., Coiro, J., Castek, J., & Henry, L. (2014). New literacies: A dual-leveltheory of the changing nature of literacy, instruction, and assessment. *Journal of Education, 197*(2), 1-18.

Livingstone, S. & Helsper, E. (2010) Balancing opportunities and risks in teenagers' use of the internet: the role of online skills and internet self-efficacy. *New media & society, 12*(2), 309-329. DOI: 10.1177/1461444809342697

Luke, A. (2012). Critical literacy: Foundational notes. *Theory into Practice, 51*(1), 4-11.

Martin, T.M. (2016, August 23). # *BookSnaps-Snapping for Learning*. Retrieved December 19, 2021, from https://www.tarammartin.com/booksnaps-snapping-for-learning/

Mesmer, H.A.E. (2020, January 23). *There are four foundational reading skills. Why do we only talk about phonics?: We must teach the integrated set of foundational skills completely*. Retrieved November 28, 2021, from https://www.edweek.org/teaching-learning/opinion-there-are-four-foundational-reading-skills-why-do-we-only-talk-about-phonics/2020/01

M. K. J. (2021, September 21). *Globalizing K-12 reading lists of children's and Young Adult Literature • Worlds of Words*. Worlds of Words. Retrieved December 19, 2021, from https://wowlit.org/links/globalizing-common-core-reading-list/

Moll, C. (2019). Elaborating funds of knowledge: Community-oriented practices in international contexts. *Literacy Research: Theory, Method, and Practice, 68*(1), 130-138. https://doi.org/10.1177/2381336919870805.

Murali, G. (2021, October 20). *On our path to global covid-19 recovery, we must focus on literacy*. United Nations. Retrieved November 28, 2021, from https://www.un.org/en/un-chronicle/our-path-global-covid-19-recovery-we-must-focus-literacy.

Murry, C. (2021, July 6). *Tiktok is taking the book industry by storm, and retailers are taking notice*. NBCNews.com. Retrieved December 18, 2021, from https://www.nbcnews.com/news/us-news/tiktok-taking-book-industry-storm-retailers-are-taking-notice-n1272909

Prensky, M. (2001). Digital Natives, Digital Immigrants Part 1. *On the Horizon, 9*(5), 1-6. http://dx.doi.org/10.1108/10748120110424816

O'Brien, D., & Scharber, C. (2008). Digital literacies go to school: Potholes and possibilities. *Journal of Adolescent and Adult Literacy, 52*(1), 66-68. ***https://doi.org/10.1598/JAAL.52.1.7***

Robinson, K. (2011). *Out of our minds: Learning to be creative*. Capstone.

Robinson, J. (2019, February 11). *Why Professional Development Matters*. National Education Association. Retrieved October 30, 2021, from https://www.nea.org/professional-excellence/student-engagement/tools-tips/why-professional-development-matters

Rodriquez, G.M (2013). Power and Agency in Education: Exploring the Pedagogical Dimensions of Funds of Knowledge. *Review of Research of Education, 37*(1), 87-120. https://doi.org/10.3102/0091732X12462686

Sales, N. J. (2016). *American girls: Social media and the secret lives of teenagers*. Alfred A. Knoff.

Sims, S. & Fletcher- Wood, H. (2020). Identifying the characteristics of effective teacher professional development: a critical review. School effectiveness and school improvement, 32(2), 47-63. https://doi.org/10.1080/09243453.2020.1772841

Stoll, L., Bolam, R., McMahon, A., Wallace, M., & Thomas, S. (2006). Professional learning communities: A Review of Literature. *Journal of Educational Change, 7*, 221-258. DOI 10.1007/s10833-006-0001-8

Taffe, S.W. & Bauer, L.B. (2013). *Digital literacy*. In B. M. Taylor & N. K. Duke (Eds.), *Effective literacy instruction: research-based practice for K-8*. (pp. 160-193). The Guilford Press.

Tanti, M. (2012). Literacy education in the digital age: Using blogging to teach writing. *Teaching English with Technology, Special Issue on LAMS and Learning Design, 12*(2), 132–146.

YouTube. (2014). *Asylum: Human Right 14—Seeking a Safe Place to Live*. *YouTube*. Retrieved December 18, 2021, from https://www.youtube.com/watch?v=Qgo7P-f5ba4.

Vasquez, V.M., Tate, S.L., & Harste, J.C. (2013). *Negotiating critical literacies with teachers: Theoretical foundations and pedagogical resources for preservice and in-service contexts.* Routledge. https://doi.org/10.4324/9780203081778

Chapter 8

Reflecting on One's Practice

Critical Literacy through the Lens of Professional Learning vs. Professional Development

Rachel Herny, Chad Knesek, and Emily Hill Ottinger

Abstract

Content-area literacies require knowledge of all aspects within a specific content area and the specific and general skills that allow teachers to effectively teach pertinent subject matter. Professional learning opportunities are where content-area literacy skills can be refined to become actionable. Social in nature, professional learning, and content-area literacy development are boosted by group interactions and collaborations rather than through lecturing and directives. In this chapter, Rachel Herny, Chad Knesek and Emily Ottinger will explore professional development versus professional learning at different schooling stages for content-area literacies. They will refine the current understanding of content literacy skills and knowledge by exploring content-area literacy at different levels. Additionally, they will address what teachers and students need in order to successfully teach and learn content-area literacy and how to identify and reflect upon the content-area literacy needs of teachers and students.

Reflecting on One's Practice: Critical Literacy through the Lens of Professional Learning vs. Professional Development

Content-area literacy entered the lexicon of education in 1970 when Herber published the book, *Teaching Reading in the Content Areas* (Dunkerly-Bean & Bean, 2016). Herber distinguishes that most reading and literacy instruction is reserved for the elementary grades, while teachers and literacy development for a specific content area takes place in the secondary grades (Alderman et al., 2013; Ruddell, 2001). While the elementary grades have a common approach, Herber was groundbreaking in the idea of merging content and literacy instruction and began to guide how teachers could use specific strategies within different content areas (Dunkerly-Bean & Bean, 2016). Therefore, the catch-phrase "every teacher is a reading teacher" at the secondary level was born. As educators, we are responsible for giving students the skill sets they need to learn our specific content area. Teachers must empower themselves to understand the intricate—and sometimes confusing—differences between the context of terminology and application. Without this knowledge, how are teachers across grade levels expected to know how to teach content-area literacy while identifying student needs within each content? We will explore content-area literacy from elementary, middle, and secondary grade levels throughout this chapter. We examine our own personal experiences, comfortability with terminology, and application of content-area literacy techniques.

Content Area Literacy

Involving the fundamentals of reading and writing, content-area literacy is where the subject matter can properly be introduced, explored, and practiced. "Content-area literacy and disciplinary literacy are umbrella terms that describe two approaches to literacy instruction embedded within different subject areas or disciplines" (International Literacy Association, 2017, p. 3). The focus of content-area literacy is on the ability to use reading and writing to learn a specific subject matter or content area (Shanahan & Shanahan, 2008). It is to be used in conjunction with subject-specific tasks to promote a complete understanding of the material. This conjunction was found to be important for students of all ages because, as readers, they actively "require various strategies when they study particular subject areas and read many kinds of materials for different purposes" (Moore, Readence & Rickelman, 1983, p. 420). At some point, though, in a student's educational career, content-area literacies develop into disciplinary literacy.

For students, literacy skills are developed over many years and continue to strengthen with practice over the course of a lifetime. Like any practical skill, basic literacy strategies are usually introduced early and increase in difficulty over time. In his comments on successfully adapting acquired literacy skills across increasingly more complex materials, Herber (1970), stated:

Like any other skill, reading skills are applied at many levels of sophistication. As students progress through the grades, they encounter increasingly sophisticated material. The concept load is heavier. The ideas are more abstract. The information load is increasingly more concentrated. …Students must learn how to adapt these skills (and even learn some new ones) to meet the demands of increasingly challenging materials. (p. 2)

Thus, not only do students need to understand the specific facets that make up content-area literacy, but they also need to have specific skills and knowledge of the content area. Within this construct, teachers play a pivotal role in providing students with opportunities to learn the reading and writing processes that are commonly employed across disciplines. According to Lent and Voight (2019), content-area literacies are the "what" whereas disciplinary literacies are the "how." Regarding the "what", teachers are expected to support their students' literacy endeavors as they "progress through increasing levels of text complexity" (Fisher & Frey, 2014, p. 348). Teachers are charged with encouraging independent practice and small group interactions centering on the skills that can be used across different content areas. Content-area literacy relies on teachers to use their discretion to make informed decisions about which strategies to teach their students, when to introduce those strategies, and how to make it work for their specific students. Content-area literacy is only as strong as the teacher's knowledge and understanding. Teachers are the experts, imparting knowledge of the how-to's and why's of the content for their students.

Teachers extend content-area literacy practices through disciplinary literacy tactics by applying those content-area skills to discipline-specific purposes. For example, an American History teacher would deepen a student's content-area literacy into disciplinary literacy by honing particular history-based skills. Such skills include evaluating and interpreting an important event, understanding the importance of a political context in a given time period, analyzing timelines/ thinking chronologically, and researching historical events. Each skill utilizes content-area literacy (being able to read and understand the text) while also needing specific, discerning expertise in what each competency requires. Educators can ensure they are appropriately extending their knowledge and understanding of content-area literacy concepts by proactively knowing to increase instructional efficiency.

They should be encouraged to look at the *whole student* to be able to identify their areas of need and plan accordingly and motivate themselves as the *entire teacher*. Trust et al. (2015) posit that the whole teacher perspective recognizes teaching as a multi-faceted and complex task that requires teachers to be cognizant, socially connected, and reflective in nature (p. 16). Educators, like students, "are whole persons—not mere collections of attributes" (Noddings, 2010, p. 5) and should be treated as such. Therefore, an effective teacher needs to have a knowledge base of their content while also being willing to be reflective in their content knowledge and teacher practice.

Early in their practice, teachers should be introduced to "extensive knowledge of content and a solid understanding of pedagogical best practices in teaching literacy" (Eller & Poe, 2016, p.17). At any stage in their career, teachers need to be cognizant of the important role that literacy plays in the classroom and "how language and content work together to construct disciplinary ways of knowing, doing, and communicating" (Shleppergrell, 2004, p. 24). For example, veteran teachers tend to rely on the same set of skills taught for generations under the guise that they are all necessary for students to be academically successful (Hadar & Brody, 2018). There is already a literacy divide amongst peers in many classrooms because many high school and middle school students are not reading on grade level (Hurst & Pearman, 2013). With this divide also comes a divide in skill and ability levels. Veteran content-area teachers tend to think that the teaching of reading is not their responsibility (Hurst & Pearman, 2013). In reality, reading and reading instruction is the responsibility of every teacher and are embedded in every content area. Students who do not understand relative terms and related activities will struggle to build content-area literacies (Rainey et al., 2017). One way to make this happen is for teachers to professionally develop their practices through professional learning.

Professional learning (PL) offers the opportunity for individuals to grow in areas of personal interest were setting their own learning goals and personal expectations are cultivated. Professional learners can develop goals stemming from personal reflections of knowledge and various educational practices (Trust et al., 2016). For example, while novice teachers are still developing their awareness of who they are and want to be in their field, more experienced teachers may be striving to improve their pedagogical practices. As teachers identify these areas of need, they embark upon a quest to find learning opportunities that best suit them. For the most part, teachers recognize a need for development in the area(s) of classroom management, content knowledge, and teacher-student relationships (Louws et al., 2017). These skills are beneficial for teachers tasked with choosing what is ultimately best for themselves and their students regarding content-area literacies.

As important as it is for teachers to benefit from professional development opportunities, there must be an effort to be thoughtful and reflective. Just as classroom assessment provides every educator a lens in which student growth is measured, personal reflection is an oft-skipped tool. Teachers, through personal reflection, have ample opportunity to celebrate their successes while also addressing weaknesses discovered along the way. Every teacher has a vision of the teacher they want to become, but striving for any goal should always involve a heightened degree of reflection. Reflection involves thinking about what one might have learned and how that learning should and will be applied in the future. The following section includes our reflections on Professional Learning as they apply to our area(s) of content-area literacy.

Elementary Level PL: Rachel Herny's Reflection

When I entered the world of education, I understood that there were so many things I still needed to learn. As a brand new kindergarten teacher, once I worked through the initial shock of having to run my own classroom, I started to realize that there were parts of my education that left gaps in my instruction... bigger gaps than I had initially anticipated. For example, my lack of foundational literacy knowledge became more noticeable as I sat in meetings with my peers. As asserted by Sulzby, Branz, and Buhle (1993) "emergent literacy includes all behaviors and concepts about reading and writing that precede and develop into conventional literacy" (Sénéchal et al., 2001). A core component of childhood education, foundational literacy includes instruction in phonics, phonemic awareness, fluency, vocabulary, and comprehension (Flewitt, 2013). Of these necessary foundational skills, I struggled to teach all areas successfully. Not only did I struggle with foundational literacy, but I also struggled with incorporating literacy into my math, science, and social studies like my principal wanted, which was a struggle. How was I going to catch up? How was I going to make a difference for my students?

When I became a teacher, I believed that my preservice institution had given me all of the tools I needed to be a successful teacher working with successful students. I believed that my school district would help me close the gaps in my own learning for the sake of my students. I was also incorrect in these suppositions. Naïvely, I believed that the professional development that my school district required me to attend was going to provide me the opportunities to continue my education so that I would become a better, more knowledgeable teacher. But after some time, I realized this was also false. I realized that my school district lacked an understanding of what I needed as a new teacher, failing to recognize and respect the agency of my professional education (Trust et al., 2016). A majority of the professional development that my school district offered was to promote their agenda across all levels of education. For example, I remember signing up for a training that was advertised to "take my classroom instruction to the next level," and it was a session that promoted a flipped classroom model. How would I reach my students in a flipped classroom when I was just trying to understand how to close their foundational literacy gaps? Additionally, a majority of the offered training were misguided, as they didn't meet any of my professional needs (OECD, 2014), they lacked subjects that engaged me as a learner, and they promoted useless topics like "How to reasonably restrain a student who is out of control" or "what to do when Danny can't sit still". Needless to say, the district's agenda was just not translating, and I found myself frustrated with the district's perception of what I needed to become a better teacher versus what I realized I needed.

It was then that I abandoned my hopes that the school district would teach me what I needed to know, and I started seeking out the most valuable resources that I had access to my peers. When I stepped back and looked around, I realized that I was surrounded by knowledgeable teachers in their grade level and subject areas. They had sixty-plus years (combined) of real-time teaching experience, and their students were all making gains toward adequate yearly progress (AYP). I realized that my colleagues could be the teacher educators that I needed, and it would be their influence and knowledge that would play a central role in advancing my understanding (Hadar & Brody, 2018). I began seeking these teachers out. I would create my own study group, participate in observations during my breaks, and immerse myself in a collaborative culture to learn through conversation with my colleagues (Trust et al., 2016). I picked their brains for tips and tricks on how to help my emergent/struggling readers across the curriculum. I would watch them in their classrooms and take down copious notes as they broke down their literacy instruction in meaningful ways for their students. They taught me how to introduce letters/letter sounds in a specific and structured order. They taught me how to structure "silent reading" time with a group of five-year-olds (the secret being to start at five minutes and increase the timer every few days—with a reward after the timer went off, of course). I learned how to incorporate science-based texts into my core reading instruction, focusing on reading strategies and science content simultaneously. I learned how a simple word problem in math could contain the word of the day, therefore reinforcing reading strategies while delivering math content. Most importantly, they taught me that while literacy needs structure, one size does not fit all. I needed to watch, listen, and observe my students' progress to make my instruction meaningful.

I was a teacher but still very much a student at this point, and my peers were the missing piece of my education. They knew how to accurately diagnose their students' misconceptions and the errors in their learning. Moreover, they could reflect in real-time and adjust their teaching as necessary. If that wasn't impressive enough, they also knew what scaffolds and safeguards to put in place so that their students would continue to receive exactly what they needed in the different subject areas. Finally, I had felt that I found my rhythm. I found who I was as a literacy teacher, and I was able to apply those lessons across the curriculum. The lessons that I learned from my amazingly in-tune peers were just the beginning of my professional learning path. Their professional knowledge and know-how prompted me to become a better teacher. Through personal introspection and deep reflection, I was able to make changes (Shandomo, 2010). I implemented their strategies in my own classroom and began being able to tweak things on the fly to make my instruction even more meaningful for my students. And while my literacy instruction transformed from a mud puddle to a deep well of information, there were still some things that were missing. As I reflected on what I had been learning, I realized that there were still areas of my instruction, namely incorporating quality literacy experiences into the other subjects, which still evaded me. I constructed meaning from what I had learned from these amazing teachers (Shandomo, 2010). I sought out book recommendations and additional, non-district required professional opportunities and began researching what made content-area literacy important and accessible. I started reading scholarly articles written by educational researchers, and I joined all of the free educator resources I could find online. Books like *Developing Content Area Literacy* by Antonacci, O'Callaghan, and Berkowitz (2014), and *Content Area Reading: Literacy and Learning Across the Curriculum* by Vacca, Vacca, and Mraz (2010) were invaluable to my success and progress. But I knew that I still needed more.

It was then that I decided to go back to school for a master's degree in Reading K-12. I felt that if I had a better understanding of reading and literacy and how those skills developed over time, I would then transfer that knowledge across the curriculum. In this, I gained a better understanding of reading processes, how students' progress through the stages of literacy acquisition, and how reading across the curriculum creates stronger students overall. Through my need for personalized professional learning, I was able to break away from what the district was telling me that I needed and truly find myself as a teacher.

Middle School Level PL: Chad Knesek's Reflection

As a freshly minted teacher, I was ready to take on the world. Surely, my undergraduate education had provided me with all of the necessary insight to establish and run my own classroom and teach in such a way that students would benefit, right? Within months of my first teaching assignment, as we all do, I realized that I had been taught only the basics of teaching and not necessarily the intricacies that result in truly effective teaching. So, how does one "fix" this very apparent lack of knowledge? We look for answers. As teachers, we instinctively seek out other teachers to benefit from the experience and expertise of those who have been in education for many years. But, even with this new knowledge from those far wiser, I continued to struggle. I found I had yet to connect the dots between my education and theirs—like identifying and trying to fill the gaps that existed in my students' learning. I quickly realized that education had continued to evolve in the midst of the time difference between our very different undergraduate educations, and I was lost somewhere in between. I knew the basics of the history of education. Still, it was in learning the evolution of education: where it had started, the changes that developed over the years (and the supporting research behind them), and where education should be headed in the future that I began to find the answers.

Surely, school districts were consistently preparing their teachers by introducing the newest, latest, and greatest advents in education, or so I had thought. As any teacher will attest, professional development is only as good as the presenter, the material presented, and teachers' need for the content. As the years passed, these sessions continued to lack what teachers needed most: to have the gaps filled in their own classroom within their learning—the dots between what used to be considered "normal" teaching and what is now the standard.

It is, in my opinion, that professional development strives to give rise to the "how" we are going to be teaching to conform to district mandates and "suggestions" as opposed to the much needed personal, professional learning wherein we are introduced to the "why."

Middle school is a fascinating dichotomy caught somewhere between what is considered rudimentary, but necessary in elementary, and that which is too complicated in high school. Having taught elementary school for eight years before the jump to middle school, I found myself on a new quest in search of the fine line in teaching that is middle school teaching. Middle-school students, unlike elementary students, are completely aware and curious as to why certain subjects and topics are taught. Middle-school teachers have all heard, "Ugh, WHY do I need to know this?" Without an answer, students are relegated to just another assignment or assessment that they feel is a complete waste of time. As I have tried to connect the dots in my own personal, professional learning, we must also connect the dots for all of our students.

It has become increasingly more evident that it is up to me to connect the dots and fill the gaps in order to ensure my students' success. For me, professional learning has taken precedence over professional development in that I am now in a place in my career where I am able to seek out and decide my own course of learning alongside that which is provided by my school. Of course, professional development is important as it strengthens a common language amongst teachers while also setting common goals. I will never forego professional development opportunities, as I have certainly learned many useful things over the years in a professional development setting, but it is my reflective spirit that has made personal, professional learning far more useful in my career.

It is the reflective teacher who is aware of their strengths and weaknesses and is willing to put in the time to hone their skills in order to share them with others who may also benefit. Professional learning grants teachers the opportunity to be more reflective than they would otherwise be able to in Professional Development settings. Of course, there is plenty of room for reflection in both, but I have found it much easier and advantageous to think about a topic that I have searched out and undertaken on my own rather than that which is expected of me by my campus. Being able to ask yourself what you think you need to learn and then going after that learning becomes a powerful tool in any teacher's arsenal.

High School Level PL: Emily Hill Ottinger's Reflection

I will never forget the epiphany I had in my third year of teaching. I attended a school literacy improvement meeting as a representative of our high school English department with a few other teachers from other departments. While trying to solve all the problems in public education and all the struggles we were having with our students, I struck up a conversation with a veteran science teacher. While discussing why students are struggling daily, this teacher flat out told me that if a student is failing my science class, I can guarantee they are also failing English. I was confused; I was still an inexperienced teacher relying on others for their expert advice to guide my classroom. The science teacher simply noted that if a student cannot read or write and fails in English, how are they supposed to read and write and master the skills they need in science? The teacher went on to denote a student's English grade is often a significant indicator of the other grades in their other classes. It was something I had never thought about. If they are struggling to read and write in English, how are they expected to master word problems in math, read passages in science, or learn a foreign language in Spanish class? Ten years later, when I look at my grade book, if I notice a student struggling with me, it does not take long to realize they are also struggling in courses other than English. Rarely is my class the only class, the student, is failing or barely surviving. While this is my own individual experience, it personally reaffirms the importance of the foundational reading and writing skills learned from elementary school forward due to what it provides in all content areas at the secondary level, as well as the value of working with other colleagues and professional learning to help address and acknowledge the literacy struggles we all need to address in our classrooms.

Moreover, the data does not lie on the challenges we face in content-area literacies at the secondary level. In 2003, data from the National Assessment of Education Progress (NAEP), also known as our nation's report card, reported that only 23% to 30% of students from the ages of ten to eighteen could read and write at proficient levels. Only 3% to 6% could read and write at advanced proficiency levels (as cited in Donahue et al., 2003). Moreover, the Operation for Economic Co-operation and Development (OECD, 2005) ranked the United States 18th in reading, 22nd in science, 28th in math, and 29th in problem-solving (as cited in Dunkerly-Bean & Bean, 2016).

A little less than twenty years later, NAEP (2020) reported reading scores for students in grades 4 and 8 are lower than in 2017, and "assessment years on the nearly 30-year trend line shows the average reading score at each grade is not significantly different compared to a decade ago... and compared to 1998, the score at grade four is higher, while the grade eight average score is not significantly different." NAEP (2020) also reported there was no change in mathematics scores since 2017. Therefore, due to the data, our students are struggling to demonstrate knowledge and competency in content areas, as well as able to apply this knowledge in real-life situations (NCES, 2021), exhibiting the need for "every teacher to be a reading teacher" as Herber (1970) suggested fifty years ago.

While this data can be daunting and defeating, those of us in education are facing these challenges on a daily basis, and in reality, we know this data to be true from our first-hand experience. Therefore, it is up to us in education, particularly as teachers who are the number-one stakeholders for a child's success in the classroom (Barnett & Arnett, 2018), to look at our content-area teaching practices through a critical lens to make the necessary changes for our students. As teachers, we are no strangers to the pressures outside stakeholders put on education and educators to perform often with unrealistic expectations. Still, we choose this challenge because we care about our students. While reflecting on our practice and content, we can help find solutions to best meet our students' needs. Therefore, in this section, I will address research and strategies I have found effective that can work across content areas, which include: blended and personalized learning (BLPL), use of assessment, need for collaboration, and need for teacher reflection over teacher practice.

Unfortunately, as teachers during professional development, we are often hit with broad data from our district or state on all the problem areas our students are facing and then simply told to go and "fix this" without any real support on what to do to repair the problem (Mandinach, 2012). While this data is valid and can help guide our practice, the data we may receive on our students comes months later. Therefore, we often have a new set of students that may bring a new set of challenges (Bedwell, 2004, Pellar, 2012; Mandinach & Schildkamp, 2021). Consequently, our own personal data we gather on our students is of far more value to address their content-area needs, but it took me a few years to realize this to be true.

A few years ago, my English teaching team received a grant to implement a BLPL classroom. As a result, I have transformed my secondary English classroom into a BLPL classroom with fundamental strategies that can be used across content areas to gather student data to address student needs which include ongoing formative assessments and one-on-one student conferencing. Ongoing formative assessments can be defined as a "wide variety of methods that teachers use to conduct in-process evaluations of student comprehension, learning needs, and academic progress during a lesson…so that adjustments can be made to lesson, instructional techniques, and academic support" (Great School Partnerships, 2014, para. 1). The purpose of the formative assessment is to change the teacher's instructional practice to meet student needs in their classroom. Without assessment, we as teachers do not have useful feedback in our hands to know how to adjust our classroom practice. It is also up to us as the teacher to decide what data with formative assessments best measure our students' needs, but this can include quick multiple choice assessment with immediate results, a simple hand raise or classroom scan, simple quick writes and exit tickets, or even a simple teacher observation to measure comprehension or engagement. I have personally found simple student observation to be highly effective. Pellar (2012) and Mandinach & Schildkamp (2021) found through their research that teacher observation and student work samples are the most valuable forms of student data and assessment.

Furthermore, I include one-on-one conferencing with students because this is where a teacher can give voice and choice to their students and hear directly from each student on their individual needs. Conferencing with my students has allowed me not to let any student fall through the cracks because each student meets with me to voice their personal needs and enhance our personal relationship in the classroom. This is also a strategy I have shared with other teachers in other departments in my school who have also found great success from simply taking two minutes of their time once or twice in six weeks to just listen. We know as educators that if we take the time to listen to our students, our entire classroom culture can change, allowing our students to feel heard and, in turn, more engaged and motivated in our classroom.

Secondly, while noted professional development can hit teachers with broad problem areas within our district or school, professional learning and collaboration is where we can genuinely hone in on developing our teaching practices based on our data as previously noted. Research acknowledges that teachers work better in collaboration and learn best from their peers (Powell et al., 2015; Fisher & White, 2016). Teacher collaboration is key to professional learning because teachers can share ideas with one another and analyze relevant data together to come up with classroom and teaching-based solutions for students' needs as my team did. Unfortunately, at the high school level, many teachers do not have the luxury of working with a team and are forced to work in isolation due to a lack of time to meet and plan, a common enemy of all teachers (Powell et al., 2015; Fisher & White, 2017; Barnett & Arnett, 2018). But sadly, without taking the time to collaborate, it can be very difficult to improve our teacher practice or enhance our professional learning.

Since I teach a state-tested subject, my district has granted my team a specialized professional learning community period where we have the privilege to meet every day. While I have this benefit now, this was not the case several years ago when my district analyzed specific state testing data and required my team to meet at least two hours a week without granting us the given time period. Of course, we were up in arms with fury for many reasons, one being they granted time for math and sciences courses but not English due to the push for STEM in our district. But as teachers often do, we complied and began meeting during our common conference and after school to collaborate as a team. In reality, it lightened our teaching load immensely. We were able to readily share ideas with each other over specific units, share what worked and did not work and why, and look at our student data to come up with solutions together instead of working on our own with no feedback. We soon realized the value in our collaboration as a team, thus giving up our one conference period did not feel as daunting as the beginning. Now, without the ongoing collaboration with my team, I do not believe I would be nearly as effective of a teacher. Moreover, even with turnover and team changes, the collaboration allows our assessment scores to improve over the school year as we better address our students' needs.

Lastly, reflection over data and my teaching instructional practice has been a huge change agent in my classroom and overall test scores. Reflective teachers are more effective teachers (Korthagen & Wubbels, 1995; Day, 1999 as cited in Çimer et al., 2013) in the classroom. The purpose of teacher reflection is to ensure our teaching practices are meeting students' needs, and if not, then the practice needs to change. Reflection is a cycle that a teacher goes through; for me, this involves gathering students' data, reflecting on the data to find areas of strengths or weaknesses, collaborating with my peers on best-fit solutions, and then changing my instructional practices based on my students' needs, and listening to them through conferencing to express their voice and choice in their learning. Then, I can reflect on whether the instructional practice met the students' needs; and if not, the practice needs to change (Children's Literacy Initiative, 2015).

While the reflection cycle can be another time-consuming process, teachers often do this automatically. Teacher reflection can occur in-action or on-action (Schon, 1983), and be legitimized by teacher reflection as a valuable source of information and knowledge (Wieringa, 2011). Reflection-in-action can occur during the midst of teaching, while reflection-on-action occurs to evaluate teacher practice (Schon, 1983). Without reflection, we cannot make the necessary changes in our classroom teachers need to be effective.

While I understand that as a high school English teacher, my goal is to share through my critical lens of content-areas literacies to provide ideas and strategies that can be used across all content areas. As educators, we are considered content-area experts, but that does not have to mean we are only of value to our given content area. Cross-content strategies and collaboration are great resources not utilized enough at the high school level due to the isolation we often feel from one department to another. It is all of our jobs to prepare our secondary students for the 21st century and to decipher the mounds of information they are inundated with daily. As previously quoted, "every teacher is a reading teacher" (Huber, 1970), we are all responsible for student literacy, but how we look at information and address literacy can be slightly different.

Closing

In conclusion, as we wrap up this section on professional and personal learning with regard to literacy across the content areas, we wish to remind our readers that education and teaching are subjective experiences and are ever-changing. We have laid out in this chapter a combination of information on professional learning and our personal experiences along the way. Some of you may breathe a sigh of relief, knowing your journey began from a much more enlightened standpoint, and to that, we say, "Well done and carry on!" Others may identify with our musings and find themselves asking, "What comes next?" as it most certainly depends on your journey. We are in total agreement that our message to you as the reader is that you must be reflective of your practice and instructional needs and allow it to guide your journey. What do you need to improve your instruction? What mode of learning or opportunities are right for you? While the answer may not be in the area of literacy across the curriculum, you might just find that your reflections have taken you to a place you never expected. As we all know, education is an adventure and knowing that there is so much to learn along the way makes it that much more exciting. Allow yourself to indulge in the adventure of professional learning, as it will surely benefit your students in the long run.

References

Barrett, S. K., & Arnett, T. (2018). Innovative staffing to personalize learning: How new teaching roles and blended learning help students succeed. *Clayton Christensen Institute for Disruptive Innovation.*

Bedwell, L. E. (2004). Data-driven instruction. *Phi Delta Kappa Fastbacks*, (516), 3.

Çimer, A., Çimer, S. O., & Vekli, G. S. (2013). How does reflection help teachers to become effective teachers. *International Journal of Educational Research, 1*(4), 133-149.

Children's Literacy Initiative. (2015, April 2). *What is data-driven instruction?* Cli.org. https://cli.org/2015/04/02/what-is-data-driven-instruction/.

Day, C. (1999). Professional development and reflective practice: Purposes, processes and partnerships. *Pedagogy, Culture & Society, 7*(2), 221-233.

Donahue, P. L., Daane, M. C., & Grigg, W. S. (2003). NAEP Reading Highlights. *Editorial Note, 5*(4), 40.

Dunkerly-Bean, J. & Bean, T. W. (2016). Missing the savior for the connaissance: Discipline and content area literacy as regimes of truth. *Journal of Literacy Research, 48(4)*, 448-475.

Eller, A., & Poe, E. (2016). *Teachers' Perception of Primary Literacy Preparation: Has it Improved?*

Fisher, D., & Frey, N. (2014). Source: The Reading Teacher. *The Reading Teacher, 67*(5), 347–351. https://doi.org/10.1002/trtr.1234

Fisher, J. F., & White, J. (2017). Takeaways from the 2016 blended and personalized learning conference. *The Education Digest, 82*(6), 42.

Great Schools Partnerships. (2014, April 29). *The glossary of education reform: For journalists, parents, and community members.* Edglossary.org. https://www.edglossary.org/formative-assessment/.

Hadar, L. L., & Brody, D. L. (2018). Individual growth and institutional advancement: The in-house model for teacher educators' professional learning. *Teaching and Teacher Education, 75*(75), 105–115. https://doi.org/10.1016/j.tate.2018.06.007

Herber, H. L. (1970). *Teaching reading in the content areas.* Englewood Cliffs, NJ: Prentice-Hall.

Mandinach, E. B. (2012). A perfect time for data use: Using data-driven decision making to inform practice. *Educational Psychologist, 47*(2), 71-85.

Mandinach, E. B., & Schildkamp, K. (2021). Misconceptions about data-based decision making in education: An exploration of the literature. *Studies in Educational Evaluation, 69*, 1-10.

National Assessment of Academic Progress (2020, December 4). *The nation's report card.* https://www.nationsreportcard.gov/highlights/reading/2019/

National Center for Education Statistics. (2021, September 5). *National Assessment of Educational Progress.* https://nces.ed.gov/nationsreportcard.

OECD. (2005). *PISA 2009 results: Executive summary.* Paris, France: Author. Retrieved from http://www.oecd-ilibrary.org/ docserver/download/9805011e.pdf?expires=1476114534&id=id&accname=guest&checksum=056EACED71702824220C5B945099DB06.

OECD. (2018). Teachers' pedagogical knowledge and the teaching profession: Background report and project objectives. Paris, France: Author. Retrieved from http://www.oecd.org/education/ceri/ Background_document_to_Symposium_ITEL-FINAL.pdf

Pellar, S. (2012). What should count for data-driven instruction? Toward contextualized data-inquiry models for teacher education and professional development. *Middle Grades Research Journal, 7*(1), 57-75.

Powell, A., Watson, J., Staley, P., Patrick, S., Horn, M., Fetzer, L., ... & Verma, S. (2015). Blending learning: The evolution of online and face-to-face education from 2008-2015. Promising practices in blended and online learning series. *iNACOL.*

Rainey, E. C., Maher, B. L., Coupland, D., Franchi, R., & Moje, E. B. (2017). But What Does It Look Like? Illustrations of Disciplinary Literacy Teaching in Two Content Areas. *Journal of Adolescent & Adult Literacy, 61*(4), 371–379. https://doi.org/10.1002/jaal.669

Schon, D. A. (1983). The reflective practitioner: How professionals think in action. Basic Books, Inc.

Sénéchal, M., LeFevre, J.-A., Smith-Chant, B. L., & Colton, K. V. (2001). On Refining Theoretical Models of Emergent Literacy The Role of Empirical Evidence. *Journal of School Psychology, 39*(5), 439–460. ***https://doi.org/10.1016/s0022-4405(01)00081-4***

Shanahan, T., & Shanahan, C. (2008). Teaching disciplinary literacy to adolescents: Rethinking content-area literacy. *Harvard educational review, 78*(1), 40-59.

Shandomo, H. M. (2010). The Role of Critical Reflection in Teacher Education. *School-University Partnerships, 4*(1), 101–113. Trust, T., Krutka, D. G., & Carpenter, J. P. (2016). "Together we are better": Professional learning networks for teachers. *Computers & Education, 102*, 15–34. ***https://doi.org/10.1016/j.compedu.2016.06.007***

Wieringa, N. (2011). Teachers' educational design as a process of reflection-in-action: the lessons we can learn from Donald Schon's The Reflective Practitioner when studying the professional practice of teachers as educational designers. *Curriculum Inquiry*, 41(1), 167-174.

CPSIA information can be obtained
at www.ICGtesting.com
Printed in the USA
LVHW080310080722
722883LV00021B/152

9 781645 042501